TEENAGERS & PARENTS:
Ten Steps for a Better Relationship

by

Roger W. McIntire

McIntire, Roger W., 1935-
    Teenagers & Parents: Ten Steps for a Better Relationship / by Roger
    McIntire.--Columbia, MD : Summit Crossroads Press, 1996.
    p.cm.
    Includes bibliographical references and index.
    Originally published: Amherst, Mass. : HRD Press, 1991.
    ISBN 0-9640558-6-4

    1. Parent and teenager--United States. 2. Adolescent psychology--
    United States. I. Title.

HQ799.15.M15 1996   649'.125

Copyright (c) 1991, 1996, 1998, 2000 by
        Summit Crossroads Press
        126 Harmison Lane
        Berkeley Springs, WV 25411
        1-800-362-0985
        E-mail: SumCross@aol.com
        http://www.parentsuccess.com

Edited by Sherry Hoffman-Blum, The Right Word

First Printing, 1991
Second Printing, 1995, revised
Third Printing, 1996, revised
Fourth Printing, 1998
Fifth Printing, 2000, revised

ISBN 09640558-6-4

DEDICATION

To Carol McIntire who provided many of the insights described in this book. Her practical and realistic approach to family problems is one of my most treasured memories. While new views and strategies are developed in this edition, her judgment and wise insights can still be recognized by those who knew her well. Working with students with special needs, Carol counseled and guided both middle and high school students and their parents from 1974 until her death in 1990.

OTHER BOOKS
BY THE AUTHOR

RAISING GOOD KIDS IN TOUGH TIMES
   Seven Crucial Habits for Parent Success

ENJOY SUCCESSFUL PARENTING:
   Practical Strategies for Parents of Children 2 -12

COLLEGE KEYS:
   Getting in, Doing Well, Avoiding the 4 Big Mistakes.

See our website for the latest parent tip and information
on Dr. McIntire's newest books:

www.parentsuccess.com

ABOUT THE AUTHOR

Roger McIntire has worked with families and teenagers since the 1960's and has three daughters, now grown with families of their own. He has taught child psychology, family counseling and therapy at the University of Maryland for 32 years. He is the author of many books including *Enjoy Successful Parenting*, *For Love of Children* and *Child Psychology* (a college text).

In addition to his work with families, he has been a consultant and "teacher of teachers" in preschools, grade schools, high schools and colleges. Professor McIntire's research publications have dealt with infant vocalizations, eating problems, strategies in elementary school teaching, and high school motivation. He also published research on college drop-outs during his tenure as Associate Dean for Undergraduate Studies.

THE TEN STEPS

STEP 1: Communicate in Positive Ways
Send Positive Messages, Get Back Positive Reactions

STEP 2: Watch Out for Blames and Games
Know Who's Responsible,
Know the Games and How to Play

STEP 3: Coach Teens about School and Social Skills
Pass Along Good Tips About School Success and Friends

STEP 4: Make Room for Your Teen to Be Useful
and to be "Weird"
They Need to be Proud of Themselves Now

STEP 5: Give Special Attention to Habits Concerning
Alcohol, Drugs, Sex, and Cars
Present a Good Model, Good Rules, and Good Reasons

STEP 6: Move Toward Treating Them Like Adults
Build Their Self-Esteem at an Early Age

STEP 7: Avoid Frequent Punishment and Its Disadvantages
What are the Results of a "Get Tough" Policy?

STEP 8: Use Alternatives to Punishment
What is a Good Adult "Get Tough" Policy?

STEP 9: Protect Your Feelings and Your Rights
Tolerate No Abuse

STEP 10: Seek Cooperation from Your Friends, Spouse
and Relatives
A Single Parent, even Double Parent, is Often Not Enough!

Table of Contents

Providing a Safe Place to Talk

Encouraging Practice of Skills They Need Now

Coaching in Critical Areas

Planning Reactions to "Almost-Grown-Ups"

PREFACE

The "teenager"stage begins at about age 10 in the U.S. It blossoms early and develops rapidly probably because of so much adult experience—second hand—from TV, CD's, VCR's, PC's, talk shows, movies, radio, and peers with similar information and misinformation.

The "teenager" stage ends when our teen shows considerate and thoughtful behavior even when near his or her parents! This accomplishment is sometimes delayed until age 30 or later!

What can parents do to help the development of their offspring during this critical decade (or two) and yet enjoy life, enjoy the family, and retain sanity for themselves? We hope to raise competent adults and afterwards continue a friendship that lasts for life. We look ahead to times when we relate to our sons and daughters as equal adults, sympathizing with each other and supporting each other.

So Step 1 begins with communication. The attitude your teen comes to expect and the messages you hope to get across make up the style and atmosphere of your interactions. The routine of these little talks deserves first place in this book. The most difficult aspects of the teen years will be more durable when the talking in Step 1 becomes easy.

When you were a teenager, how did you feel about yourself when you were talking with your parents? Were you a competitor, part of the opposition, or did you feel befriended by an advisor who was on your side?

Most parents love their kids. But when we were growing up, many of us were not sure our parents *liked* us because their day-to-day focus often ignored our good points and focused on our mistakes. This made us unwilling to take the risk of making an effort to talk with our parents.

So Step 2 takes up an advanced aspect of talking with a teen: Who gets the blames and who gets the credits?

Steps 3 to 10 lay the groundwork for allowing teens to practice the competencies we hope they will acquire in school, social situations, home, and in managing their responsibilities.

The early onset of some competencies in some teenagers is a challenge because teens are becoming *over*-prepared. Ready for life in some ways but with few opportunities to show their maturity. The most dangerous situation on our planet is a human being with nothing to do. What will he/she be allowed to do?

The 10 steps describe practical strategies for *everyday* parenting of teenagers—with the crucial expansion of their responsibilities built in. These steps are about teaching, coaching, setting limits, and then, finally, about building a pleasant situation where both teens *and parents* are comfortable.

The goals of all ten steps are:

1) to raise a teenager to become a competent adult;
2) to have all the family members enjoy the family; and
3) for everyone to remain close friends when the job is done.

Providing a
Safe Place
to Talk

STEP 1
Communicate in Positive Ways

The most important question your teen will ever ask is, *"Mom (Dad), can we talk?"*

If your teen gets the right answer to this question, all the other steps in this book will be easier, and your adult experience will be available to your teen at a low price. So go slowly here and thoroughly review your conversational habits with your teen.

Conversation Rule #1:
People (Especially Teens) Dislike Evaluation

Many people, especially teens, are most interested in themselves. They tune in to the parts of conversation that are about them, and they are less interested in the rest. The most important part of the conversation will be, *"What does the message say about me?"* A talk with your teen can go sour immediately because we parents think the *topics* are the most important parts while our teen reacts first of all to *personal evaluation*!

TAKE ONE:

> *"You should have seen what happened in gym today, Dad."*
> *"What, Donald?"*

*"Keith got in an argument with Mr. Effort, and they ended
    up in a real fight!"*
"I'm sure it wasn't much of a fight."
"Yes it was. They were wrestling!"
"I hope you didn't have anything to do with it."
"Naw, all I did was cheer."
*"Cheer? Listen, Donald, you'll end up in trouble right
    along with Keith! Don't you have any more sense than to
    . . ."*

Let's interrupt Dad here just for a moment. Dad criticized his
son's story: (1) he thinks Donald was wrong because it wasn't
much of a fight, (2) he thinks Donald probably had something to
do with it, and (3) he thinks Donald shouldn't have cheered.

Dad centered the conversation on what he disliked about his
son's behavior instead of the story. All this happened in a 20-
second discussion. Donald, like all teens, will resent the way his
dad turns his story into a talk about the mistakes that Donald made.
In the future, Donald will drift further away and Dad will get less
and less information.

Your style of communication tells your teen how you feel
about him or her at the moment. This is the most important part—
not the topic, and here's the first point of possible misunderstanding and conflict. A teen extracts this personal evaluation in less
than a sentence. If the signals are negative, up come the defensive
reactions before any useful exchange begins.

Let's back up and give Dad another chance to be more friendly
and yet still communicate the possible consequences of the gym-
class experience to Donald.

RETAKE:
"You should have seen what happened in gym today, Dad."

"What happened, Donald?"

"Keith got in an argument with Mr. Effort, and they ended up in a real fight!"

"How did it all start?" (Dad ignores the possible exaggeration, doesn't express doubt, and shows interest instead.)

"They just started arguing about the exercises, and Keith wouldn't give in.

"Hard to win against the teacher." (Dad comments in general and suggests alternatives that are not critical of Donald.)

"Yeah, Keith is in big trouble."

"Did they ever get around to the exercises?" (Dad is interested in the story, not just in making points and giving advice.)

"Keith was sent to the office and then we tried these safety belts for the flips. Do you know about those?"

"I don't think we had them in my school."

"Well, you have these ropes..."

Donald has a clearer view of the incident now and understands the hopelessness of Keith's argumentative attitude. He wasn't distracted by having to defend himself when he told Dad the story. And now he's explaining something to his father. Dad's positive evaluation of Donald comes through in his respect for him and interest in what Donald is saying.

Conversation Rule #2:
Use "It" Instead of "You"

When Dad gets his second chance, he says, *"How did it all start?"* One habit that helps avoid the instant evaluation pitfall is keeping topics on an "it" basis. When a conversation seems threatening to your teen, try to look at a problem as an "it" instead of "you" or "me." This tactic avoids the trap of "attack, defense, and counter-attack." Conversation does not make a good competitive sport.

TAKE ONE:

Mom: *"How was art class today?"*

Amy: *"Oh, OK, what I saw of it."*

Mom: *"What do you mean?"*

Amy: *"Mrs. Clay sent me to the office."*

Mom: *"What did you do?"* (Attack.)

Amy: *"I didn't do anything!"* (Defense.)

Mom: *"You must have done something; you aren't sent to the office for nothing!"* (Attack #2, conversation going badly.)

Amy: *"You never think it's the teacher's fault; you always blame me."* (Counter-attack, looking for a way out.)

Mom: *"What kind of talk is that? Let's have the whole story."* (Attack #3, conversation almost destroyed.)

Amy: *"Oh, nuts!"* Amy stomps out. (Conversation dead.)

Mom can do better by avoiding the personal evaluation (Rule #1) and using the 'It' topics of Rule #2.

RETAKE:

Mom: *"How was art class today?"*

Amy: *"Oh, OK, what I saw of it."*

Mom: *"What do you mean?"*

Amy: *"Mrs. Clay sent me to the office."*

Mom: *"WHAT happened?"* (Emphasizes "it" instead of "you." IT happened. This is better than, "What did you do?")

Amy: *"Tom ripped my paper."* (The conversation takes a new turn with Amy's answer to the "it" question.)

Mom: *"Oh no!"* (Emphasizes sympathy rather than an evaluation of the mistake.)

Amy: *"Yeah, so I shoved him."*

Mom: *"And so she sent you to the office?"* (The focus is on facts and sympathy instead of taking advantage of a chance to reprimand something that's already been punished at school.)

Amy: *"Yeah."*

Mom: *"Then what happened?"* (Good "it" question that avoids "let's get to the bottom of [your mistake in] this!")

Amy: *"Well, for one thing, I'm behind in art again."*

Mom: *"Well, if you can stay away from Tom, maybe you'll catch up. What else happened today?"* (Mom adds a little parental advice and then on to looking for someTHING more positive)

The opportunities to "teach a lesson" and "fix the blame" are temptations most parents find hard to resist. But sometimes the benefit of getting more facts outweighs the "quick-fix" or "make-them-sit-up-and-take-notice" approach. People who avoid instant evaluation and defuse confrontation with an objective conversation of "it" topics are easier to talk to. They are interested in the other person's experiences, not in placing blame or emphasizing mistakes.

Conversation Rule #3:
Use Reflective and Sympathetic Statements

Often a teen's first remarks are only an expression of feelings and are short on facts. If parents jump in with advice or opinions and little information, their reactions could be way off target.

Reflective statements are useful ways to hear the teen out. The reflective statement says nothing new and only repeats what the teen said in different words. Without adding anything new, this agreement keeps the conversation going and provides opportunities to get straightforward information without defensiveness. The parent only repeats what the teen said while showing sympathetic understanding. Reflective statements take a little creativity to avoid looking simple-minded or manipulative, but in small

> *If parents jump in with advice or opinions and little information, their reactions could be way off target.*

amounts these reactions can allow teens to continue *their* topic of conversation. Let's look at an example of reflective statements in action by a mother learning about her daughter.

Amy: *"Man, is that school boring!"*

Mom: *"It's really getting you down."* (Mom is reflective and just uses different words for "you are bored")

Amy: *"You bet."*

Mom: *What's getting you the most?"* (A good it-question starts with *"What,"* instead of, *"Why are YOU so bored?")*

Amy: *"I don't know. I guess it's the whole thing."*

Mom: *"You need a break."* This is reflective of "the whole thing (is boring)" and is a sympathetic remark that avoids, "There must be something wrong (with you)!" which would be threatening.

Amy: *"Yeah, but vacation is six weeks away."*

Mom: *"Got any plans?"* (Good, puts the conversation on a positive topic.)

Amy: *"No."*

Mom: *"Hard to think that far ahead."* (A reflective statement that just repeats "No plans" with sympathetic words.)

Amy: *"Pam is getting some applications for camps."*

Mom: *"Sounds like a good idea."* (Avoids the quick evaluation of, "Camp might be expensive...it might be too early to apply, etc." Immediate negative evaluations only discourage the search for answers at this early stage.)

Amy: *"I might ask her about it."*

A complaint about boredom such as this is a familiar remark to most parents. Although not much is solved about boredom in this conversation, Mom has a better understanding of her daughter's feelings and has avoided the temptation to "get something done" in this short talk. Indirectly, Mom said she has had similar feelings to her daughter's, and it's all right to have those. Most important, it's all right to talk to Mom about feelings without being criticized for feeling bored.

> **Because Mom allowed her daughter to direct the topic, information flowed to Mom.**

By allowing her daughter to direct the topic, information flowed to Mom, and she has a "ticket of admission" for next time:

"Say, did Pam ever get any camp applications?" or,

"Only five weeks left now; how's it going?"

Notice there is no room for adding old complaints in this approach. Avoid frequent criticisms such as, *"You shouldn't be so negative,"* *"You don't plan ahead like Pam"*, or out-of-left-field complaints such as, *"You're always sloppy!"* *"You never do your homework!"* and *"You have bad friends!"* Such criticisms are too broad and will be taken personally because they say, *"And while I'm thinking about you, another thing I don't like is..."*

Instead, encourage the teen to take the conversational lead and postpone parental topics. The other steps in this book will deal. with those other complaints.

Conversation Rule #4:
Help a Teen Explore Alternatives

Reflecting a teen's statements can help the teenager get to a point of exploring alternatives to a problem and taking action to solve it. When a parent sends the message, *"I heard you,"* and *"It's all right to feel the way you do,"* the teen is likely to go beyond letting out feelings to considering, *"What can I do about it?"*

A parent helps most by tuning in to the teen's level of feeling and energy. Is the teen looking for alternatives, considering a particular one, or just letting out emotion? The parent must listen with empathy and react appropriately to give support. If the teen is getting rid of emotion, a helpful parent reflects that. At other times a teen may not have figured out alternatives but may want to.

> Megan: *"Those kids are always teasing me. I don't know what to do."*
> Parent: *"What alternatives are there?"*

Teens are creative at listing options when they are ready. But if no idea comes up the problem may not be clear yet and the teen needs to explore more by expressing opinions and feelings.

Perhaps Megan is ready to try an alternative.

> Megan: *"I'm going to tell those kids to quit bugging me!"*
> Parent: *"How do you think they'll react to that?"*
> Megan: *"They might stop, but if they don't I'll just*

> *ignore them from now on."*
> Parent:　*"Just ignore them?"*
> Megan:　*"Yeah, that works every time!"*

Well, the ignoring strategy may not work all the time, but Megan is now encouraged to take control and is working on her own problem—that's a step forward and a step toward growing up.

Distinguishing different teen levels of emotion and energy and reacting with support requires practice and empathy. When in doubt resist the temptation to suggest solutions.

Conversation Rule #5:
Avoid Suggesting Solutions too Soon

Parents are always tempted to suggest solutions to problems: *"Why don't you . . ." "You should try..." "Don't be so . . ."* These statements are well meaning, but they often strike the listener as being pushy and superior. Most of us don't react kindly to suggestions for quick solutions.

> *Most of us don't react kindly to suggestions for quick solutions.*

If you told me you're frequently late for work because of traffic, and I said you should get up earlier, you would be offended. I was just trying to be efficient and give quick advice, and parents often just want to fix things—preferably quickly, but efficiency in conversation is for business meetings and TV shows—and not for the family.

Family conversation should be enjoyed; it's not a job to get out of the way so we can get on to really important stuff. Teens need a place to talk to you, too. As one lonely teen put it to me, *"If all they want is a successful project, why don't they take up a hobby?"*

Why does your teen resent your long phone conversations with friends? Because you tie up the phone and take too much time from them? Yes, but they may also resent the friendly, non-efficient nature of your conversation with your friends that doesn't come through when you talk with your teen. As an example of overcoming the temptation to fix things too quickly, look at the following conversation:

> Sarah: *"Life is so depressing. People are so bad."*
> Mom: *"I know it gets like that at times."*

Here's a good start. The topic may seem like a bad place to begin, but it's Sarah's choice. A terrible start now would be for Mom to fall to temptation and disagree right away by trying to *"set her daughter straight"* with the solution: *"You shouldn't talk like that; there are a lot of good people in the world!"*

This correction is tempting but unnecessary—Sarah knows her remark is extreme. Also, it's dishonest on Mom's part because she knows Sarah is partly right. Since the statement has some potential for agreement, Mom's reflective statement takes the side that puts her a little closer to Sarah. Let's see how it goes:

> Sarah: *"It gets like that all the time at school."*
> Mom: *"There must be some times that are good at school."*

Not good, Mom's saying, *"You're wrong."* It's too early in the conversation for the implied disagreement, authority, and solution expressed in this nudge. Let's take that back and try again:

> Mom: *"School's been bad lately, huh?"*

This is better because it's reflective without evaluating who's to blame; it keeps the conversation on a third entity where Sarah started it (not her fault; not Mom's). The next remark from Sarah is likely to be informative about what the problem is at school.

Mom, if careful, will learn a lot and Sarah will *"get it all out."*

In most conversations between adults, the suggestions for solutions are left out completely. We don't end up a conversation with a neighbor by saying, *"So we're agreed you'll cut the hedge at least every two weeks!"* or, *"So don't go roaring off in your car like that, it disturbs everyone!"* If those statements are familiar you probably don't see much of your neighbors!

Be satisfied that most conversations with your teen, like those with your neighbor, will have few immediate results. Leave out the closing comment in most of your conversations. If you try to be the "winner" in every talk, then you will always have to make someone a "loser."

Sending Messages about Loving a Person; About Liking a Behavior

Most parents love their kids, even their teens, but they may not like some of their behavior. *"I love them, but I don't always like them and it comes through."* You can't like anyone's behavior 100%, but you can't always be a critic either. After the insult of the criticism, your teen will be gone, and the conversation will be over. Not much accomplished in that.

As parents react to what their teens do, the messages of not liking this and that accumulate. These messages can overwhelm the less frequent expressions of love. It's important to be sure that your reactions are sending the right messages.

Mom: *Leave baby brother alone, Justin.*

Justin: *I was just going to pat him.*

Mom: *I know what you were going to do. Now just stay away, you will wake him!*

Mom: *I like to pat him, too. But it will just wake him up and he's tired.*

Justin drops some crumbs from his potato chip bag.

Mom: *You are so messy!
Look what you did!*

Mom: *Oh, look what hap-
pened! Better pick
those up so they don't
get trampled into the
carpet.*

If Mom chooses the comments on the left, she emphasizes Justin, the person. *You* will wake him, *you* are messy. If she chooses the comments on the right, she emphasizes a third thing that *she and Justin* are dealing with together: *It* will wake him.

> *Over the long haul, Justin ends up with a very different message and a very different relationship with Mom.*

Look *what* happened. **It won't make a lot of difference to Justin on this one occasion. But over the long haul, Justin ends up with a very different message and a very different relationship with Mom.**

The emphasis on the defects in the person act as a punishment. Jovial and approachable people never seem to punish. They have a rule that says, *"When mistakes happen, emphasize outside events"* (such as Conversation Rule #2, above). To the extent that they must correct, contradict, reprimand, and punish, they risk losing this friendly air. **This can be one reason some growing daughters and sons become alienated from the family and would rather go outside with friends or stay in their own rooms. The likelihood of criticism, "put downs," and corrections drives them away—just as it does adults.**

Mom and Dad:

> Mom: *"John, sometimes I wonder if you really like me, you criticize me so much!"*
>
> Dad: *"Honey, I <u>love</u> you. You know that."*
>
> Mom: *"Yes, but you never compliment me."*
>
> Dad: *"What? You want gush and mushy stuff all the time?"*
>
> Mom: *"No, I just want the benefit of the doubt. I want someone on my side, on the lookout for my good points and my successes; I've already got plenty of critics in my world!"*
>
> Dad: *"You have <u>plenty</u> of good points."*
>
> Mom: *"Then point them out now and then."*

Praise, encouragement, and genuine friendliness are no doubt the most effective influence spouses have. And the same good influences work on their children, too! When positive attention is used consistently in a direct way for particular behaviors, we get results. **It cannot be emphasized enough how much your positive attention influences your children and others.**

Teens engage in a conspiracy—almost unconsciously—to show you that you are having no effect. They don't have the insight or assertiveness to have conversations like the one above between Mom and Dad.

But don't be misled. It may not show up in the short run, but your reactions to your teen's behavior do make *the* difference. Don't give up. Watch a certain behavior for a few weeks to test your influence and notice how upset teens can be when they feel ignored! Attention, praise, and general encouragement are handy rewards. They should be used often.

Selecting behaviors for positive attention is the main business of being a parent. Use your good sense and the exercises in

this book to keep your attention on target. Your habit will be
contagious and the whole family atmosphere will be more positive.

> *Selecting behaviors
> for positive attention
> is the main business
> of being a parent.*

If looking for mistakes becomes the
routine, parents are on the road to a
habit of correction, reprimand and
punishment. They become unpleasant
and don't like themselves when doing
the parenting job. A teenager will
respond in kind and avoid the family situation when possible.

Friends and Searchlights

Friends bring out the best in me. When we meet, their attention sweeps the common ground between us looking for sparkles to
highlight. I like the "me" they draw out. I return the compliment,
like a friendly searchlight, seeking the best in them.

Parents and their sons and daughters should be friends. Not in
the sense of enjoying the same music or having friends in common,
but through enjoying time together and supporting the strengths
and successes in each other.

Some people have another focus. Their search overlooks the
good in me and zeros in on vulnerable spots. I pull back and risk
very little because I know what they're looking for. I cover up.

Aim *your* searchlight carefully. What are you looking for?

Why the Messages May Sour

The good in some people is hard to find, and your inclination
to criticize can easily out-weigh any temptation to praise. In
families, it's not always the child's or teen's behavior that is so
wrong. Part of the problem may be a parent's lack of good defini-
tions of right and wrong.

We parents know very well what bad behavior is: making messes, being disrespectful, yelling, fighting, etc. But the words we use for good behavior are often less specific: "be nice" and "act right." **Not having an exact idea of what good behavior should be, we have trouble finding it.**

The search is more difficult if "good" is described by what we *don't* want: *"don't make trouble, don't yell at your sister, don't sulk and slam doors just because you're annoyed."*

Descriptions with "not" and "don't" in them are hard to use. *When* should you react to *"not* fighting" or *"not* sulking?" And when these rules are finally learned, what is a teen *to do*? What should a parent look *for* in his or her teen's behavior? Better to think of specifics— help with setting the table, saying some-

> *Not having an exact idea of what good behavior should be, we have trouble finding it.*

thing complimentary to your sister, helping your kid brother practice his soccer. Vague expectations about good behavior and specific descriptions of bad, can lead to a common situation of unbalanced parental reactions with bad behavior attracting most of the attention.

We are quite sure that bad language deserves criticism or punishment, but our positive expectations of a "good attitude" are vague. This emphasis on the negative can lead parents to think of themselves more as police officers than as moms and dads.

Without specific positives to look for, parents send fewer positive messages. Even the vague supports that occasionally surface, *"You're a good kid!"* and *"You're doing all right!,"* have such unclear targets that they don't influence anything in particu- lar. *"Don't talk like that!"* *"Straighten up!"* and *"Clean up your mess!"* can be frequent and specific, but so frequent that the general message is *"you're bad."* We need to select specific positive targets to avoid too-frequent criticism. I asked one dad to give me some specifics about his complaint that his daughter, Kim, was "messy." I thought he could be more helpful by deciding the specific actions he *wanted* her to perform. He said, *"I want her to make her bed, put dirty clothes in the laundry hamper, pile her belongings on wall shelves, and dust and vacuum her room."*

Instead of accusing her of being "messy," or commenting on the whole person of his daughter, he used the list to direct attention toward these specific actions. By focusing, he could take one step toward specific changes in the behaviors he felt were important.

> *Without specific positives to look for, parents send fewer positive messages.*

Also, Dad could begin to plan when he could praise instead of bringing up the old complaints like, *"you're messy"* that may be interpreted as, *"(I don't like you), you're messy."*

He chose the best time to talk with Kim about the work, decided on the level to expect from her at first, and was ready with his approval and other rewards for her effort. Then he began to look for ways to encourage improvement in her performance.

My experience with Ryan is a good example of sour messages; Ryan came into our office waiting room and first sat on a convenient chair; Mom chose to sit at the opposite side of the seating area. *"Sit over here,"* she said. He moved to the seat next to her. *"Don't swing your foot like that!"* Ryan picked up a magazine from the table. *"Be careful with that,"* she said. He turned a page noisily. *"Shh, I _told_ you to be careful!"*

As it turned out, one of the complaints from both teachers and Mom was that *Ryan* was bossy and constantly critical of others! Mom had developed low expectations and low tolerance, and it was contagious. In turn, Ryan developed his own habit of being critical of others.

Routine Strategies, Routine Results

The problem illustrated by Ryan's mother is almost always the result of a lack of planning. The critical part of planning that is left out is determining which behaviors are important and which are trivial (see Exercise 4, p. 120). Had Mom ever thought about whether Ryan should always sit next to her? She said she had not. Why had she told him to do so? She said she was afraid he "might do something wrong over there." She said she had no *specific* fear he would do anything wrong, she just didn't trust him. Some boys might deserve such distrust, but for Ryan it was just habit with a little reprimand thrown in. **A psychological leash had been put on, and it was jerked regularly.**

To break the habit of the psychological leash, a good rule is, *"Don't correct or instruct your teen until you are certain a mistake is being made."*

This is the rule that all adults expect you to apply to them, and your teens deserve the same treatment until they prove otherwise. Mom (or Dad) should train herself/himself to hesitate before reprimanding, correcting or discouraging a behavior that is not worth the trouble.

When Ryan's mom tried the *"catch 'em being good"* suggestion, she told Ryan how well he was doing on a part of his homework and, another time, how well he had cleaned up his room. He said, *"What's the matter with you?"*

In the second week, after a few more compliments, Ryan's reaction could melt your heart. *"Do you <u>like</u> me?"*

> *A psychological "leash" can replace the teen's responsibility for his own behavior.*

he asked. Mom said, *"Of course, I do."* And Ryan said, *Wow."*

The psychological leash is worth breaking for additional reasons. Corrections that are intended as reprimands may become rewards over a long time. The leash replaces the teen's responsibility for his own behavior. He just does what he wants while he depends on his parent to make all the corrections. **So while striving for perfection, total dependence is achieved!**

A Message to the Teenage Nag

The corrections with the psychological leash may come to be learned by teens as a nagging strategy they can use on others. All parents know this drill very well. It's the nagging that never dies!

> Rachel: *"But Mom, why can't I ride to school with*
> *Nathan?"* (Rachel is 13.)
> Mom: *"I already told you why, Rachel."*
> Rachel: *"I know, but pleeease! Nathan's a good driver."*
> Mom: *"No. He just got his license and driving to school*
> *is just asking for trouble."*

The next day it starts all over again:

> Rachel: *"Mom, Nathan wants me to ride with him to the*
> *mall, can I go? We're not going near school."*

What events maintain Rachel's behavior? It's a topic that brings disagreement and punishment, but she brings it up anyway. The first and most likely reason for this running battle is that Mom and Dad have never held a brief planning session about the problem. Without this planning session, the reasons given to Rachel change from time to time; her parents disagree from time to time; and they lose confidence in these decisions from time to time as details (mall or school) change.

The inconsistency encourages Rachel to keep trying because one day she thinks she might hit the right combination of

details and get to go. She probably will.

The planning session would nail down the reasons, pinpoint the agreement between Rachel's parents and give them confidence. It would help by stating the honest reasons for the decisions in detail.

> Mom: *"Your father and I have decided you may not ride with boys to school or on errands without an adult. We think other students will get in on it and make trouble whether it's school or anywhere else. When you are 15, it might be all right. Right, David?"*
>
> Dad: *"Right."*

Now will Rachel stop nagging? Probably not, but the amount of nagging will decrease, and Rachel will be a little happier because the situation is now clear, honest, and fair—at least Rachel's parents think so, and it gives them confidence. For Rachel, the structure makes the situation more comfortable than the continual argument, although it's still not what she wants. Rachel's argumentive behavior will mellow because the statement of the rule is concrete and detailed—not much room for loopholes.

> *A planning session helps parents feel more in control and less vulnerable.*

Rachel's parents should not be discouraged because there is no dramatic change in the argument. The planning session is to make them feel more in control and less vulnerable to the nagging. Rachel is not going to be satisfied on this topic until she gets what she wants, probably when she's 15 or older. But her parents can be a bit more comfortable knowing they have an agreed-on policy.

As the air clears, Rachel's parents need to stay alert and make a special effort to engage her in conversation and encourage her. They don't want this vacuum to fill up with other unwanted nagging.

What Kind of Day Will They have Today?

Good parental strategies, such as the consistent rules of
Rachel's parents and the focus on positive behavior that Ryan's
mother needed are habits with important benefits. Parents sometimes develop different habits when dealing with their kids than
they use when dealing with adults. Rather, they come to expect
something different from children and worry about the slightest
deviation from their expectations. But often the expectations
themselves have never been thoughtfully worked out.

**What at first appears to be a high standard of behavior by
Ryan's mother turns out to be actually** *no specific* **standard at
all.** So a parent in such a situation punishes (in mild ways) nearly
everything and finds no opportunity to reward good behavior.

One teacher I talked to was surprised that Ryan was having
problems, *"I know he can be difficult, but I have decided to catch
him doing well. I focus on finding his good moments and when I
find one, I let him know it. I think he knows I'm giving him a
chance and that I like him."*

Adults expect the same of us, more tolerance, more chances to
make amends for mistakes, and we show them a better disposition.
What is expected of us, and what we expect, create the social
atmosphere we live in. The adult rule is, *"Don't correct or reprimand until a mistake has been made. Certainly withhold punishment, it creates bad feelings."* Here's one reason the atmosphere
is better in the teachers' coffee room than in the hallway.

Another teacher I know said that as she went down the school
hallway, she noticed classes reacting to teachers in ways that were
"typical" of each teacher's classes. She was surprised that students
could make such quick adjustments as they went from Math to Art
to Gym, creating a recognizable atmosphere in each place.

From a selfish point of view, if you were the parent or teacher of these kids, how would you like to spend your day? With teens who are modeling positive behavior or teens who are modeling punishment?

So how shall we encourage? **The most effective reward we use is verbal praise and encouragement.** When praise is consistently used in an obvious manner for a particular behavior, results are gratifying. An additional improvement comes when the attitude is imitated. Some parents and teachers may devalue the effect of their positive attention because they only briefly observe an immediate target activity. In the longer view however, a teen's disposition will become a close copy of the surrounding adult attitudes.

Give **a nice day.**

Exercise 1: Practice the Conversation Skills

Practice the rules of Step 1 with another parent or a friend while you share a simple story such as getting the kids to school or helping them with homework. Begin with one person as the listener and one as the teller.

Review these guidelines for good listening.

1. **Keep frequent eye contact.** Look at your conversation partner most of the time. A teen expects a good listener to look at him/her. We don't like to feel unattended because the person we're trying to talk to is staring at the newspaper or TV while we ask a question. Teens feel that way too.

2. **Use good posture.** Face your teen while talking and listening. Use body language that says, *"I'm alert! I'm interested!"* A parent who slumps, looks away, or even walks away sends messages that discourage and insult the talker.

3. **Avoid criticism and ask questions.** Use questions that continue the conversation by asking for longer answers than just *"yes"* or *"no."* *"How did it feel?"* is more likely to continue the talk than *"What time was it?"* Emphasize *IT* questions instead of using *YOU*: *"How was it at school today?"* not *"How did you do at school?"* Careful questions can help in a neutral, non-opinionated way, so the person asking the questions gains a better understanding of what happened and why.

4. **Avoid solution statements and use reflective statements.** Re-word the last thing your partner said to show you understand what he/she told you. *"Boy, I really hate that Mr. Jones for math!"* could be answered with, *"He really annoys you"* or *"You get mad in there a lot, I guess."*

   Replace the temptation to give advice or criticize by reflecting your partner's statements instead. Suggestions such as *"Why don't you . . .?"* or *"Have you tried . . .?"* make the talker feel inferior, resentful, and argumentative. You will get the whole story by reflecting. Your listening helps because the speaker will clarify the situation and his feelings by telling you about them.

5. **Share your experience**. Share stories, jokes, and experiences that helped you learn about getting along in life. Be selective, avoid stories that are too close to a sore point with your teen. If your son or daughter feels your experiences are not directed as advice to his\her specific weaknesses, the tales can be enjoyed, and they will improve the relationship.

STEP 2
Watch Out for Blames and Games

Positive communication promotes more comfortable and informative conversations with your teen. But through the processing and maneuvering going on in your family, you will go beyond conversation to the complex negotiations of parenting. This step points out some dangers in placing blame and giving credit in parent-teen negotiations, and stategies teens are tempted to use.

Who Deserves the Blame and Who Deserves the Credit?

We usually give credit for successes, but for mistakes and failure, we distribute the blame in one of two ways: For *our own* mistakes we usually choose "outside blame" that finds the explanation in circumstances outside of ourselves. This makes us unfortunate victims of situations outside of our control, *"It was so noisy there, how could anyone think or be able to do the right thing?"* "Outside blame" also includes people, *"I was too dis-*

tracted because people were coming so late!"

When it comes to the mistakes of *other people (including children),* we are tempted to use "inside blame." *"What* (inside condition) *makes him so inconsiderate, so clumsy? Why doesn't she pay more attention? What was she thinking of?"*

Inside blame is a dangerous habit. Parents should use it carefully. It leads them to frustration and inaction because the teen is viewed as "having" (inside) an almost unchangeable character.

Outside blame leads parents to look for problem *situations* instead of problem *kids*. **With a good understanding of a problem situation, you have a chance to discover a workable solution, and that, in turn, gives your *teenager* a new chance.**

> *Outside blame leads parents to look for problem situations instead of problem kids.*

In order to plan reactions to problem situations, you need a clear view of what's happening. Blaming the teen doesn't help because it makes assumptions about what is going on inside. For example, the complaint that Nicholas is *"too demanding and selfish"* refers to real actions of Nicholas, but also implies the problem is part of his nature. The result is that the blame has been put inside Nicholas, and his parents may believe that any change can only come from there.

Nicholas: *Dad, can you drive me to soccer practice now?*

Dad: *Just a minute, Nicholas, I'm listening to your mother.*

Nicholas: *Oh great, if I'm late for practice, I won't get to play on Saturday.*

Dad: *Just a minute!*

Nicholas: *We need to leave right now!*

Dad: *A minute ago you were watching TV, now we have to drop everything and rush.*

Nicholas: *Forget it. I just won't go.*

Dad: *You just said ...*

Nicholas: *I mean, I'll just skip Saturday, too.*

Dad: *Just get in the car, OK?*

Nicholas: *OK, if you insist.*

Dad: *What!?*

Later:

Dad: *That kid is so selfish. He sits around watching TV, then demands immediate service because <u>he</u> was late! And then, he blames me for insisting he hurry! This switching the blame drives me crazy!*

Mom: *Maybe he is selfish, but we could try a rule that says all rides require a 5-minute take-off time. And any time he tries abusing us like that we should just say, "Well if you really don't mind not going, OK!"*

Dad: *You're right. Soccer is less important than giving him the message he can't twist us around like that.*

Mom: *It might not always come out perfect, but at least we will take back a little control of the situation.*

Instead of fixing the blame (he's selfish), Mom suggested they try changing their reactions to Nicholas when he makes a demand. It could be he's doing it for attention and even an argument about his demanding nature could be rewarding.

The *"Why?"* of a teen's behavior is best answered by changing *"Why?"* to *"What happens next?"* Nicholas makes an

inconsiderate demand and then what happens? His ride comes
through *and* any disruption is blamed on Dad for not cooperating
on demand.

> *The "Why"*
> *of a teen's behavior*
> *is best answered*
> *by asking,*
> *"What happens next?"*

What different consequence could
be planned? The answer is never
simple and obvious, but Mom starts
at the right place by looking for a
solution instead of blaming
Nicholas. This approach is more
productive than giving up and just labeling him "selfish." The new
focus may lead to a plan to support Nicholas' considerate behavior
and to exercise caution in reacting to his little traps.

Parents should be on the lookout to give credit for the good
accomplishments of their son (or daughter), but they often feel
these opportunities are few and far between. The problem may be
partly due to the way behaviors are described. If good behaviors
are only vaguely defined, they are less likely to occur and be
recognized. Deciding just when to support a teenager may not be
easy:

Matt (age 13): *I got my room cleaned up.*
Dad: *Great!*
Matt: *I didn't pick up the parts to my model
because I'm not finished with it yet.*

Here's a crucial moment for Dad. His choices are: continue
support for what was done; after all, half a loaf is better than none,
or hold out for a higher standard and only give credit when the
whole job, with the model put away, is done and the credit is due.

A definition of what is acceptable would help; doesn't Matt
have the option of leaving one on-going project out? Matt's
parents will have to make this judgment of Matt's progress and

potential, but **the parental habit here should be to err to the side of support—there are few circumstances in adult-rearing where there is a danger of an overdose of support.**

Another concern for Dad is what kind of credit should he give. "Outside credit" may be "no credit" (support) at all for Matt: *"I guess the mess finally got to you. Even you couldn't stand it any more."*

So Dad shouldn't give the credit to Matt's environment for driving Matt to do the right thing, and Dad shouldn't take the credit himself by saying, *"Well now, didn't I tell you that would be better?"* Dad should send the credit directly to Matt for getting the job done:

> Dad: *Well, you still need the model out; you would have to just about wreck it to put it away. You (not me, and not other influences) have it looking really good in here!*

Looking for Needs and Wants Instead of Blame and Credit

Recognizing the priorities of needs can sometimes explain the otherwise puzzling fate of some rules. For example, I worked with two very different sisters whose reactions to cleaning up their rooms were very confusing.

Michelle needed to be constantly assured that her parents thought she was capable and successful, and she tried hard to be cooperative and helpful. Her sister, Susan, also seemed to value her parents approval but wanted prolonged attention and companionship more than praise.

A rule that reminded their mother to praise both daughters for keeping their rooms nice worked well for Michelle seeking praise but since attention ended when her room was done, attention-seeking Susan procrastinated in doing her part just to keep the cleaning going on and on. Susan prolonged the room-cleaning chores for the attention she received—even negative attention would do—while our more goal-directed Michelle worked hard for the confirmation of her success.

Mom may want her daughters to clean up their rooms to keep the place looking nice, but does she have to be right on top of them while they do it? The reason may be that while she thinks having a nice room is the point of the clean-up (a long-term goal), the daughters' priorities may be quite short-term—one wants assurance that she is contributing (doing it right); the other wants attention for doing any work at all!

Mom has *two* strategies to work on. One strategy Mom carries out deliberately—encourage them when they clean their rooms; the other strategy is an unintentional one of giving unusual attention to Susan's procrastination. So Susan *slows up* for attention, but Michelle *finishes up* for praise.

The solution for Michelle and Susan's mother came with the insight that Susan needed attention at the end and long after the chore was completed. This attention did not need to be in the form of praise for room-cleaning; it just needed to continue in order to show Susan that finishing the room didn't finish Mom's attention.

It would be a mistake to conclude that Michelle wants to please Mom and Susan doesn't. Or that Susan just wants to aggravate her mother. These conjectures about sinister Susan would only lead to more nagging and a sour turn in Mom's relationship with Susan. Mom is the adult and *she* had to make the special effort, after room-cleaning, to show interest in Susan.

The Temptation to Increase the Blame as They Grow Up

As children become teens, blaming them is increasingly tempting for parents, *"They're old enough to know better!"* This habit can distract parents from looking for a chance to give personal credit when it is deserved. For example, you might know a teenager who is moody, disrespectful, rebellious, or cynical. This might be a "long-standing habit" (inside blame) and his parents may think, *"That's just the way he has always been."* But even older children act the way they do partly because of the way they are treated—because of what has ordinarily happened next.

> *Teens may act disrespectful because that's the only time they are taken seriously.*

Teens may be disrespectful because the only time they are taken seriously is when they act disrespectful, or their bad behavior may produce an entertaining argument, or **their bad talk may seem more "adult" than saying something pleasant. Even some adults believe that!**

When the disrespectful teen turns happy and cheerful, adults may pat him on the head and tell him he's a "nice boy" but otherwise ignore him. The usefulness of bad behavior in this situation is not lost on the teen.

Showing respect for your teen by asking for his opinion, showing confidence in his abilities, and doing a good job of listening will bring out an improved form of respect in return. This strategy, an example to be modeled, encourages an attitude that will replace "disrespectful."

> Dad: *It's too early to start the garden outside, but we could start seeds inside. What do you think, Dustin?*

Dustin: *What good would that do?*

Dad: *Later, when you plant them outside, they would have a head start.*

Dustin: *Even melons and stuff like that?*

Dad.   *Even melons. Let's do melons.*

Is a "Game" Going On?
What Game Are You In?

"Don't play games with me!" an aggravated parent will say. But everyone plays a few games, and the best step in dealing with a game is to recognize what the teen's purpose is in the game and how you want to play it.

Game 1: *"Referees Are Fun"*

Steven: *"Mom! Mark won't turn down his music!"*

Mom: *"Mark, turn it down. Steven needs to get his homework done."*

Mark: *"He's not doing his homework, he's just goofing around with it."*

Steven: *"Mom! Mark still has it too loud!"*

Mom: *"Steven, it sounds OK to me now."*

Mark: *"Mom, Steve came in and turned off my music!"*

Steven: *"Mom, Mark pushed me!"*

Mark: *"To get you out of my room, I have to push."*

Mom: *"You two cut that out! Mark, get out here right now! If I have to come in there..."*

In this game, Mom is referee. You can almost hear someone yell, *"Hey, Ref! Call those penalties and control the game!"* It's safer than regular conflict because you can count on Mom, the Ref, to call a halt to the escalation. By the way, as all basketball and soccer mothers know, referees are always wrong 50% of the time from each player's point of view. **So if you lose, you can always blame the referee—what a comfortable way to pass time or procrastinate on doing homework!**

Why don't adults play this game? Sometimes they do, of course. It's just that the third party referee can't be counted on to keep the game going or to intervene when the conflict gets hot. Once the referee leaves the game or fails to play the role of protector, the players have to quit or start negotiating.

Most referees are tempted to coach now and then and parents are no different: *"Mark, why don't you let Steven do his homework and play the music later?"* The argument may continue but at least the suggestion puts responsibility on the players—that's why suggestions are usually resented. But coaching is more comfortable for a parent than being referee.

> *Many of these games become less troublesome to parents when they identify the game and change their reactions to give control back to the teen players.*

If the suggested solution is rejected, Mom could always end the game by removing the source of the conflict—Mark's music or Steven's selected place for doing homework. If Mom remains stern, she might insist the boys use one of her solutions. The danger here is that if Mom is not stern, her solution will only become a new source of "fun and games."

The resolution can't be perfect for the kids. But Mom's goal here is to get herself out of the referee role and give responsibility back to the boys. The less-than-perfect solution can be fixed any time the brothers want to fix it. **Many of these games become much less troublesome to parents when they identify how the game is being played and change their reactions to give control back to the teen players.**

Game 2: *"I'll Bet You Can't Make Me Happy"*

Here is a game that also pulls the parents into the problems of
their teens when the teens should be taking responsibility.

> *"Mom, what can I do, I'm bored."*
> *"Why don't you finish your art project?"*
> *"I've done most of it, and it's not coming out right."*
> *"Well, how about helping me with dinner?"*
> *"That's just work."*
> *"Well then, you might as well get your homework done."*
> *"I don't have to do it yet"*
> *"Well, why don't you..."*

Many parents recognize this conversation as one that could go
on and on. There's a continuing attention from Mom as long as no
suggestion is right. As a matter of fact, if a suggestion were
accepted, the game would be over.

Suppose old hard-headed Uncle Harry and his friend, Al, came
over and started this game with you? **You would probably make
a few suggestions, and then since they are adults, you would
think it was time for the old coots to entertain themselves!**

Parents can't win the *"I'll-bet-you-can't-make-me-happy"*
game, but after a few suggestions, they can pass the responsibility
back to the kids.

Game 3: *"My Problem is Your Problem"*

This is a common game of young teens that will develop in
later teenage years into *"It's Your Fault Because You're My
Parent(s)."* **As with many of these games, frankly stating the
fair truth may stop the game and allow some real progress.**

> *"This homework is due tomorrow, Mom!"*
> *"Well, you'd better get at it, Tyler."*

> *"Where's some paper?"*
> *"In the desk."*
> *"I already looked there."*
> *"Why don't you try upstairs?"*
> *"Mom! It's supposed to be down here."*
> *"Could you go look?"*
> *"Hold it, Tyler, your homework is your responsibility. Don't make it my problem."*

> **Frankly stating the fair truth may stop the game and allow some real progress.**

This game has a little of the flavor of the *"I'll-bet-you-can't-make-me-happy"* game. In both cases parental attention looks suspiciously like the reward that's prolonging the game, and it's time to put Tyler on his own for awhile to search for solutions.

Game 4: *"You're the Parent, Let Me Tell You Your Job"*

Alan: *"I'd like to take those self- defense classes, Dad."*

Dad: *"Good exercise. And it could come in handy."*

Alan: *"Well, the ones I want to take are in Freetown."*

Dad: *"Freetown? That's almost an hour from here."*

Alan: *"Sam is in the class near here, and I don't like him."*

Dad: *"I can't drive 2 hours every Saturday because you don't like Sam."*

Alan: *"You're supposed to help me. There's no other way."*

Dad: *"You could take the lessons here."*

Alan: *"You're the Dad. You're supposed to take me!"*

Dad: *"Alan, I'll be glad to take you to the lessons here, but I have a life on Saturdays, too. I'm not driving to Freetown."*

Alan's game brings up the important notion that Dad has the
right to be selfish at times. Alan's tactic of telling Dad what his
responsibilities are isn't working, and he may change the game to:

Game 5: ***"If You Serve Me, I Won't Make You Feel Guilty"***
    Alan: *"David's father drives him to Freetown."*
    Dad: *"Well, I don't have that much time."*
    Alan: *"Time for your own son?"*
    Dad: *"Alan, don't start that. You know I spend a lot of*
           time with you on our projects."

Well, this is not going well for Alan and if he doesn't think of a
good argument fast, he's going to have to take lessons locally.
Alan may have to start yet another game:

Game 6: ***"I'm Not Responsible, You Are Guilty***
             for My Mistakes"
    Alan: *"Well, don't blame me if I get in a fight with Sam."*
    Dad: *"What?"*
    Alan: *"You're making me take the lessons here, so if I get*
           into trouble it's your fault."
    Dad: *"Alan, <u>you</u> are responsible for what you do. If the*
           situation with Sam is that bad, maybe you should
           skip the lessons."

Alan is almost out of ammunition for this argument and is in
danger of having to show responsibility and consideration for Dad.
He can't have his own way, and like the rest of us, he resents
having to compromise and make some extra effort to get along.
What tactic is left?

Game 7: "You're Not Right, Because…Because"

Alan: *"Dad, it's not that far over there."*

Dad: *"It's the other side of the interstate!"*

Alan: *"The lessons here are not as good."*

Dad: *"You haven't tried any yet."*

Alan: *"They might be more money here."*

Dad: *"Call and find out."*

Is Alan going to call now? Probably not. Before he agrees to do that, he may ask Dad to make the call, bring up Sam again, and he may get out a map to show Dad he's wrong. Eventually, Alan will realize Dad is not driving to Freetown.

The key here is Dad's firmness for his own welfare without attacking Alan with, *"You're inconsiderate, irresponsible, selfish, etc."* Dad sticks to the issues, *not* Alan's personal traits.

Game 8: "If You Really Loved Me, You Would Serve Me"

Here's a game that is similar to the *"My-Problem-is-Your-Problem"* game with a little extra pull on the guilt strings of Dad or Mom.

Michael: *"Mom, I need those shoes!"*

Mom: *"Michael, I told you. You have a pair of running shoes—one pair is enough."*

Michael: *"But these are different. Matthew's mom got him a pair."*

Mom: *"I said one pair is enough—it's too much money."*

Michael: *"Matthew's mom said they're worth it for <u>her</u> son!"*

Mom: *"Michael, don't run that guilt trip on me. I'm the one who bought you the first pair remember?"*

Calling Michael on his attempt to blame his mom for his troubles will not stop this argument, but when Mom recognizes the game, she can keep the proper view of the talk and not let her *son* get control of *her* emotions.

If the reasons (current consequences) for the game are hard to find, perhaps you haven't looked far enough. Possibly some chain or group of behaviors is performed before the consequences occurs. For example, complaining about school only results in the parents' suggestion of what to do about homework, which provides an opportunity for procrastination about it and then a game of *"I-haven't-got-this,-get-me-that."*

The school complaint is a secondary means to the teen's goal—a step along the way to getting the parent tangled in the homework responsibility. Consider the teen who fights and complains about his siblings in order to get his parent to referee and then separate them. He now has a short entertainment entitled *"Referees are Fun,"* followed by getting the room to himself.

Game 9: *"I May Do Something Bad!"*

"I may do something bad" is a game where the teen *talks* about wild intentions because of his parents' intense reaction. When you suspect this game you can try to inhibit your strong reactions to his verbal description of his intentions and concern yourself only with performance. These are important strategies to work out in your planning sessions and in your parent support group (see Step 10 on some ways to get this going). Without a strategy, the teen finds it easy to "get through" to you by making a remark about some absurd behavior he has no intention of performing.

In the *"I may do something bad"* game, getting a teen to "talk right" sometimes becomes the goal of the parent and the power struggle for the teen. **Little talks may become unproductive, because if the teen starts to lose he can always say (promise)**

what is being demanded without having to carry it through.
Threats may be made, voices raised and your teen may get a good
"talking to," but he will only learn to say what is expected and to
avoid any genuine discussion of controversial topics.

Game 10: *"You're Just Not Perfect!"*

Here's a game played by both parents and teens. Parents will
push for perfection while hoping to produce a stronger motivation
in their teen:

Mom:	*"Sandra, don't forget to practice your flute before dinner. I think you could be really professional some day."*
Sandra:	*"BORinnng! I'm sick of it. Why are they so particular about the way you hold it?"*
Mom:	*"Don't start arguing. Just get in there and get busy."*
Sandra:	*"I think I'll work on the computer for awhile first."*
Mom:	*"You were so excited at first and now you don't practice for days. What happened?"*

Everyone starts projects that later falter. Why would a
daughter procrastinate on practicing her music when she was so
excited at first? Why would she keep missing practice by letting
the hours go by? It's time to support smaller steps far short of
"really professional" and Mom needs to be content with Sandra's
less than perfect dedication to the project rather than risk giving
attention to the procrastination.

If the goal of music lessons is enjoyment of music then the
little steps along the way are the ones to encourage; the pursuit of
perfection was never the purpose. Has her attitude toward music

been raised? It's hard to know. All one can do is support the
activity and set a good example through interest. Since progress
toward a concert debut was never the point, why not just join in her
interest and forget perfection? Often you may be accomplishing
more than your teen would like to admit.

Sandra can play a version of *"You're-just-not-perfect"* also.
Her purpose may be to belittle her parent's influence or power, or
she may just have a negative attitude. The habit can fool a parent
into thinking nothing is getting done:

> Sandra: *"These art museums are boring."*
>
> Mom: *"Some of these paintings are very famous and beautiful."*
>
> Sandra: *"They're all old pictures of old people."*
>
> Mom: *"But look at this one. Can you see how the artist used light and dark to show how the light comes from the candle?"*
>
> Sandra: *"I could do that."*
>
> Mom: *"And look at this one. Look how some things are made to look far away and some closer."*
>
> Sandra: *"They're just smaller."*
>
> Mom: *"But they are just the right sizes, and a little less clear."*
>
> Sandra: *"I guess."*

Is Sandra getting a new appreciation of art? Be careful in
concluding that Sandra's museum trip is a waste of time just
because she thinks it's not the "perfect" place to go. **Remember,
sometimes kids feel an obligation to make you believe you are
not having an effect!** Later on, when Sandra encounters other art
or tries out her own painting skills again, you may get a better
indication of the usefulness of the museum trip. **Keep your own**

spirits up on the museum trip even if things are not going perfectly, and guard against following your teen's gloomy attitude. More may be getting done than either of you realize.

Regardless of your approach to child-rearing, or adult-rearing as I like to call it, the question of whether anything has changed in the mind of the child will remain partially unanswered. All parental efforts will seem only partly successful. Teenagers, seeking proof that they are persons in their own right, want it that way!

Listening During the Game

Good parental listening skills are crucial to handling games that teens play. All the rules of Step 1 apply here. When the conversation starts, look at your son or daughter rather than a TV screen or newspaper. To deal with any of these games you need to focus all of your attention on it. Turn and face him or her so that there is no impression that you will miss what's really going on. These physical aspects of your attention let him or her know that you're paying attention and are not likely to be fooled by a game.

Feedback of what your teen just said is a good habit during these conversations. Let him or her know that you heard what he or she said by repeating it. Avoid suggesting solutions in these games. They only lead to *"make-me-happy"* or *"my-problem-is-yours."* Also, suggesting solutions makes you sound superior and tempts your game-player to counter with something different just to stay even.

> *Every time you make a winner, you also make a loser.*

Take up the habit of asking questions in a form that is not threatening and don't try to "win." Parents who frequently try to win by getting their son or daughter to *say* they'll try harder, be more responsible, or not be bad any more, may feel some progress has been made. But every time you make a winner you have to make a loser and the next conversation is likely to be more confrontational as your teen tries to improve his or her record.

Taking All that "Guff"

One obvious characteristic of a teen's "bad disposition" is that it generally reduces parent demands. It's true that a parent can silence a teen or keep him from acting up by taking a threatening pose that implies punishment. The teen learns and uses the same idea, but since he is a less powerful figure he must use threat in a more subtle way.

I have named a teen's threats and lack of compliance "Guff" or "Guff Control" because some parents I have worked with said they had a habit of giving in rather than *"taking all that guff."*

> *Some parents give in rather than take "all that guff."*

Your teen might use guff to put you off and to get out of undesirable requests for work. But his behavior also is a result of the fact that the request is *just* work; that is, he is using guff to avoid a job because the job itself doesn't seem to pay off.

By this time you may be getting a little tired of the idea that everything has to pay off. But remember that what we mean by "pay off" in many cases is just the honest expression of appreciation or admiration or support when something good or helpful is done. Material reward is not always necessary. In your job you probably do many things because you believe that it is the right way to do it or that it will please someone. You did it for some reward that had meaning for you, not necessarily money.

Guff control is usually a reaction to too little pay off, and it is continuous because it attracts some attention of its own. Now if it also works in getting out of some requests, we are well on the way to building ourselves a real problem.

Why don't you try guff with your boss? Because it wouldn't work, I would bet. And also with a good boss, it never occurred to you to use guff because there *is* a consistent support for doing the job—pay, appreciation, or some combination of both.

So Sam, at 14, usually engages in guff; his parents try to bring about some effort from Sam by coercion; and he avoids that effort—if he can—because it is straight coercion without a significant reward.

When Sam is using guff, he often exposes the situation quite well by saying, *"Oh, why should I do that anyway?"* The statement is pure guff intended to stop a request from Mom or Dad, but, incidentally, it asks a very good question: *"What does Sam get out of it?"*

One difficulty is that attempting to coerce behavior is much easier than planning and providing support for an alternative—as any boss would tell us. Providing reasonable, positive consequences requires planning and sometimes a new point of view that at least includes opportunities for more social approval.

When the Game is Over, Watch for a Chance to Encourage Something Better

Children, teens, and adults learn by doing—by practice. When the game stops, what activity will fill the gap? They will practice something, so we should encourage good selections. Practice allows trial and error in the protection of the family where parental encouragements can consistently motivate more practice and emphasize the benefits of better behavior. If parents work out more exactly what is happening and what they want to happen, then they can apply this fundamental law of learning: *"One learns what one does!"*

Anyone who has ever tried to play a musical instrument, improve in a sport, or raise children knows that just talking about it is not enough. Readings and lectures and memorizing rules can help, but real practice is crucial! Even golf has helpful hints and rules to learn, but all golfers know the only way to improve is through practice. And all golfers know players who still search for the magic gadget or secret technique for success

> *The main role of a family is to provide a place where successful practice is supported and mistakes receive only constructive reactions.*

while they avoid practice time. **The notion applies equally well to social behavior, controlling anger, getting along with siblings, homework, tooth-brushing, and money management!**

So helping a child listen and pay attention to advice is not enough, he will have to try out your instruction, test your rules, and then, if the consequences and encouragements are there, he will learn. The progress itself—the result—will have to come from practice. **That is the main role of a family—to provide a place where successful practice is supported and mistakes receive only constructive reactions—not a likely experience in the outside world.**

Careful Messages for Daughters and Sons

Parent expectations of sex differences are revealed in their questions and opinions of teen behavior. Different versions of *"You're-just-not-perfect"* can expose a sexual bias you didn't know you had! Bias can reduce the self-confidence of a girl interested in an area traditionally "masculine." It can also delay development of social skills in a boy if he is excused from social

Girls	Boys
Are you happy?	Are you successful?
Are you acting right?	Did you win?
Is your homework perfect?	Is your homework done?
Is your hair attractive?	Is your hair combed?
Are your shoes shined?	Where are your shoes?
Don't eat too much.	Don't eat too little.
Sleep, you look tired.	Sleep, you act tired.
Exercise to look better.	Exercise to be stronger.
Have friends.	Do sports.
Be friendly.	Be competent.
Be attractive.	Be productive.

obligations because he's "a naturally immature boy." The bias can slip in early, be on the lookout for it. Note the gender biases in the table above.

In spite of the recent emphasis on gender equality, our expectations of boys and girls differ; boys and girls develop different capacities and motivations, and the world has different expectations of them. Whether the characteristics are inborn or learned, I'm sure you needed no table to recognize the left-hand column above as the one for girls and the right-hand for boys.

We emphasize different values for boys and girls, and different aspects of growing up, partly out of consideration for them and partly out of our desire to prepare them for a world we know still has sexist expectations. Sometimes our emphasis is in the best interest of the child or teen, sometimes not.

Parents usually react to a boy by directing him toward success with the tasks at hand and by placing less emphasis on social relationships. Usually we encourage girls to succeed socially and give only the necessary minimum emphasis on the task at hand.

Pressuring boys about being winners and girls about being perfect produces stress that will be resented. It also risks a reaction by your teen of proving your values wrong, *"I don't have to win* (or be perfect), *and I'll prove it, I'll quit!"* A parent who pushes for a perfect student or a perfect charmer may end up with a school or social dropout.

Encourage Teens of Both Sexes to Try New Skills

The job for parents and teachers is to carefully separate fact from prejudice. A teen needs to be encouraged to try many skills, develop interests and abilities into strengths, and enjoy successes. The sources of sex differences are in both the environment and our heredity, and there are real differences. Records of school problems with males reflect these different averages for the sexes. Of course, car insurance companies know about these sex differences too.

The parent's role is to avoid unrealistic expectations and unfair limitations created by sex stereotypes while remaining alert for opportunities to help teens learn by practice. Taking a risk and trying out new tasks may be influenced by the teen's self-confidence, partly acquired from parents. Sex biases of parents will partly determine how much practice a teen will risk and, in turn, how much encouragement a teen will experience.

"OK," the gym teacher said, *"Everybody make two lines at the side of the exercise mats. If you want to practice the standing exercises, get in the line near the windows. If you want to practice handsprings, line up over here."*

Donna's friend: *"Come on, Donna, I'll help you with the flip."*
"Flip?"
"The handspring. Com'on I'll help you."

> *"You can get hurt doing that."*
> *"You can get hurt getting off the bus!"*
> *"Naw, it's mostly boys over there. Anyway I'm not very*
> *good at that sort of thing."*
> *"OK, but I'm going over. Mr. Effort said I'm getting pretty*
> *good for a girl."*

So Donna's friend went to do handsprings and Donna started for the floor exercises. Floor exercises were boring to Donna, but she felt safe with her own gender and safe from embarrassing mistakes.

Donna's expectation of herself determined what she practiced, and her expectation grew from many seeds planted by parents and teachers. There was a choice and she decided to practice merely what she did best—a habit many of us have. She was intimidated from trying handsprings perhaps because of adult implications. Or perhaps she has learned from experience that she doesn't have the athletic ability for handsprings and would be hurt trying. Certainly kids have the right to apply their own common sense!

> *Donna's expectation of herself determined what she practiced, and her expectation grew from many seeds planted by parents and teachers.*

But if her timidity came from cautions and lowered expectations suggested by adults merely because she is a girl, then she has been tempted away from her potential, and another opportunity to gain self-esteem has slipped by.

Did Mr. Effort really tell Donna's friend she was pretty good *"for a girl?"* Or was the sexist qualification presumed by a girl who has become wise to the ways of the world? Whether spoken or presumed, she's a strong person to focus on the encouraging part of the remark and continue her practice.

Let's look at a male example:

> Teacher: *"Today I want to check the sketches of plants*
> *you started outside yesterday."* The art teacher
> starts to visit from desk to desk.
>
> Jim: *"Hey John, let me have one of your sketches to*
> *show Mrs. Aesthetic."*
>
> John: *"Use your own, Jim."*
>
> Jim: *"Com'on John, I only need one. I threw mine*
> *out when we came in yesterday—I'm no good at*
> *this nitty-gritty stuff."*
>
> John: *"Do another. She won't be here for a while."*
>
> Jim: *"I told you, I'm no good at this nitty-gritty*
> *stuff!"*
>
> John: *"You don't even try, Jim."*
>
> Jim: *"Oh yeah? I'll see you outside!"*

Has a boy like Jim, who says he's no good at "nitty-gritty
stuff," been sold on his own weaknesses by a prejudiced society?
Is he "no good" because he lacks potential, or has he been
convinced he is "no good" by the same sexism that told Donna to
stick with floor exercises?

Encourage Enjoyment of Success

Mom and Dad stop to pick up their two teens from school.

> First Teen: *"I got my math papers back today, and I got*
> *more right than anyone!"*
>
> Dad: *"Wow, that's great. I hope you'll have time*
> *this weekend to study so you can keep ahead*
> *of the others."*

> First Teen: *"Oh, I can keep ahead of them easy."* (Does the competitive attitude tell you this person is a boy?)
>
> Dad: *"Just knuckle down to it and you'll get it."*
>
> First Teen: *"I have another decimals assignment tonight."*
>
> Dad: *"Well, if you want to stay at the top, you have to keep at it."*
>
> Second Teen: *"Mrs. Brown said we have to choose a final project for home economics: a cooking or sewing project."*
>
> Mom: *"Cooking can be fun."*
>
> Second Teen: *"My friend Jennie is doing cooking, but I'm better with sewing."*
>
> Mom: *"Wouldn't you rather be with Jennie?"*
>
> Second Teen: *"I guess you're right."*

Regardless of the sexes of these two students, one is encouraged to be concerned with success, while the other is encouraged to be comfortable.

Questionnaires about adult attitudes toward children tell us that the person in the math class is likely to be a boy, and the one who is encouraged to worry about friends before projects, a girl—at least the parents are treating them that way. There is no mistake here, merely an example of common family conversation where parents should be sensitive to their own reactions. Then they can encourage each teen to develop his/her very best potential, without too much concern for fitting into common molds.

How Will Others Treat Your Children?

Most people will not treat your kids any better than you do!
You set the tone for your friends and relatives on how you want the
kids treated, and the adults tend to give them the same respect and
have the same expectations you present.
These other adults will also react to the collection
of skills, presumptions, and attitudes your teens
have acquired *from* you. In your childhood, *your*
expectations were partly acquired from *your*
parents' attitudes and the foundation of your self-

> *Most people
> will not treat
> your kids
> any better
> than you do!*

concept was begun. Now you are passing along that information—
those assumptions about the good in yourself and the good in
others—modified by the valuable experience you are willing to
add.

From that, your children will develop an expectation about how
others will perceive them. This becomes a self-fulfilling cycle of
expectations because they have acquired a whole pattern of
attitudes, assumptions, and habits that will tend to *re*create in new
acquaintances, the same experiences they left behind.

Most people won't treat your children any *worse* than you do,
either! People model each other, and their reactions tend to create
their surroundings. **Each of us cause some people to fade away
and others to draw closer. We feather our own social nest.**

Your teens will pick up your model of how you treat each
person. They will pick up your attitude, disposition, and the nature
of your appetite for life. Then they will be off to create their own
social environment by reacting in ways you would find familiar.
Without giving it much attention, they will present a certain model
to others that they acquired from you. And from what is reflected
back, they will select people who confirm their expectations.

I find this responsibility to present a good model the most

awesome responsibility of parenting. The requirements of care, food, clothing, and schooling are tasks we come to handle each day. But the image that I constantly present before my children is a continuous responsibility. None of us feels completely successful in this task.

The business of parenting is to "handle" the children and influence their habits directly and by model. Those lessons, taken together, teach more than skills. They teach your teens what to expect *of themselves.* **So your children learn from your social style and the life philosophy it represents. They learn from your model the way you handle problems in the family *and* they acquire an attitude toward themselves.**

Exercise 2:
What Are Your Teen's Interests,
Abilities, and Successes?

1. **List your teen's interests and abilities shown so far.** Give a few examples of the many areas where time and effort are spent: school subjects, sports, hobbies (cars, nature, art, writing, cooking, music), social activities, organizations, and working or playing with younger kids.

2. **List ways you can help your teenager have a realistic self-concept about his/her abilities.** Recognize your teen's help with plant care, balancing a checkbook, fashion decisions, or child care. *"Tom, you definitely have a way with kids. What is it you do that makes them come to you?"*

3. **Describe how the activities have been encouraged.**
   Example: Camping—encouraged interest in camping by helping her camp out in the backyard and make out summer camp applications. Finally, she was encouraged to plan for a trip with two girlfriends to a local campground.

4. **What successes have been enjoyed in each area?**
   Examples: Bicycles—recognized by friends who asked for help repairing theirs.
   Sociality, math ability, and honesty—encouraged and complimented when he was chosen as treasurer of a school club.

5. **Has your teen expressed interest in any areas in which you limited him or her solely because those areas didn't fit the usual sex roles?**
   Examples: Dancing—son wanted to take dancing lessons, but his parent said dancing was a sissy activity. Golf—Judy was interested in golf, but Mom said there wouldn't always be

someone to go with because not many girls played golf.

6. **In what ways can you help extend your teen's abilities?**
   Drums—A mother rented a drum set to expand practice time
   for her daughter who then was able to use her energies to
   create, rather than hang out with friends who allowed few
   chances to develop creative interests.
   Swimming—Dad drove his son and daughter to swim team
   events even though they were sometimes two hours from home.
   Both became teen lifeguards the following summer.

This exercise highlights the importance of developing a wide
range of preferences and potentials that a teen enjoys and does
well. The choices a youth feels are successful can be the ones that
bloom into a career or lifelong recreation.

A listing under item 5 points to a need for re-evaluation of your
decision. The parent role is to avoid limiting the young adult's
choices by sex stereotypes and to encourage the youth to try many
skills.

The parent can help the teenager realistically see his/her
interests and abilities as they develop into strengths. Evaluate
activities and purchases that can help your teen strengthen abilities.
The goal is to discover the largest range of activities possible and
for your teen to grow toward independence.

Encouraging Practice of Skills They Need Now

STEP 3
Coach Teens About
School and Social Skills

As their children reach early teens, some parents are surprised at how much guidance and practice their young teens need. School and friends begin taking up almost all of a teen's time and attention and just a little coaching from parents can be a long-lasting help for a teen struggling to adjust to everything at once.

SCHOOL SKILLS

Adults looking back realize that school success was a critical ingredient of happiness in their child and teenage years. Comfort and success in school strengthens the teen's self-image and parents' satisfaction. If you can help your teen in this important part of his or her life, what a gift it is! And that success provides more than confidence in academic abilities, it influences feelings of competence and usefulness outside of school as well.

Looking back again, we all remember how we compared ourselves to schoolmates and reached an impression of them and a judgment *of ourselves as well*—possibly before we were 10, but certainly during our teen years. Parents who have attended their own school reunion after a few years know how the reunion seems to measure us against that old bench mark again. **This common reaction to reunions demonstrates how important help in school is to a child becoming a teen.**

> Greg: *"Mom, I don't want to go to school anymore."*
> Mom: *"What? I thought you liked school."*
> Greg: *"Well, it's boring and a lot of it doesn't make sense."*
> Mom: *"Getting along in school is hard. What part do you do best?"* (Mom shows good listening skills in order to hear the whole story.)
> Greg: *"Best? Oh, Math, I guess, but what good is it anyway? And in Geography I just can't remember all that stuff and the kids in there don't like me anyway."*

School is such a large part of a teen's life that if it isn't going well, it clouds almost all other activities. Greg pointed out several sources of trouble when he said he was bored because he didn't see the use of math, couldn't remember the geography, *and* "the kids don't like me." Let's start with Greg's boredom.

Providing Answers to, "Why Should I Do That Stuff?"

Kids who say, *"It's boring"* could be sending a confusing message. They could mean that interest is low, and they don't see the need, or they could mean they are bored because they can't keep up or, the opposite, they are too far ahead. Parents need to sort out these different meanings before they react.

The poor student who finds school lessons of "no use" usually means he finds no importance *for him* in the tasks that are requested: *"Why should I do that? It's just busy work."* A parent could be misled at this point and start explaining why *she*, the parent, thinks the work is important.

> Mom: *"Math is important, Greg, because one day you'll have to manage your own money and figure out shopping and many other things in life."*
>
> Greg: *"Uh, yeah."*
>
> Mom: *"Also, you need it for the higher math that will get you into college."*
>
> Greg: *"Higher math? There's higher math??? I think I won't go to college."*
>
> Mom: *"Don't talk like that. Of course, you want to go to college."*

The "one-day-you'll-need-these-things" approach to this problem is not on target with Greg's original objection. His point was that the work is not important *for him*. Greg's value of the "you'll-need-it-for-college" argument is revealed when he suggests giving up college just to avoid math problems tonight!

Mom needs an approach to the meaningfulness and importance of a good education that is within Greg's short-term view of the world. It won't help to provide more arguments about, *"You can't get anywhere without a good education,"* or, *"Jobs will be harder to get, promotions will be harder to come by, and you'll end up with a hard life!"*

At the moment—in the short run—Greg doesn't want to, or can't, deal with those things. The *"getting anywhere"* idea is too far in the future and too abstract—anyway the people on TV seem

to do all right, and some of them don't have much education. And
how much education would a person need to earn the amount of
money that *Greg* would think is plenty?

So why should Greg study decimals tonight? What use is it
to know portions of Geography or American History? Why is
spelling important? The answers need to be in the present activities of Greg's life. Remember he's a person with short-term
priorities.

> *New skills learned at school should be encouraged at home.*

As he gains new skills from school each
day, he should be encouraged to use them at
home. Sometimes that requires real creativity by the parent. Could Greg use his math
to keep track of the family checking account? Receive a fee for doing so? Could
Greg handle the grocery list? Take the money and do the shopping? Will he make costly mistakes? Yes. **Couldn't he just stay
interested in this stuff until he needs it? Probably not.**

One mother I work with shows how such skills are useful by
taking her 13-year-old son to the bank with her. She allows him to
go in alone and pay the bills. When he returns with the correct
change and explains it all, she gives him a "tip." The "tip" is a
parental judgment call and might not be necessary for many boys
who would be happy with the importance of the task and trust they
were given, but **her son will never ask why he has to know math
—he knows why.**

He also bakes for his mother. And when recipes need to be
halved or doubled she does not interfere in the calculations. From
bitter (and sour) experience he knows the importance of these
skills. And he feels a little better about his own worth. **He's not
just a kid, he's a kid with useful skills that his parents respect.**

Many skills not covered in school are also important to learn.
Cooking, washing clothes, caring for your room, and later on, car

care. All tasks present opportunities for teens to learn and gain a feeling of self-esteem as they become competent. The chores may be domestic ones that adults shun or view as burdens, but they still have the potential of letting the teen be productive and helpful *now*.

Parents may need to show great tolerance as they allow practice with these important school-related tasks or tasks of everyday drudgery that parents could do faster. Calm your impatience with the knowledge that just mastering the task is rewarding and insures the further benefit of a little self-pride. Mistakes are easier to tolerate because the benefits of pride and competence form part of their child's protection against later temptations of self-abuse—drugs and alcohol, for example.

> *Mastering a task is rewarding and insures a bit of self-pride.*

When the task is closer to drudgery than to adventure, more enthusiastic praise will be needed. Ordinarily a person gains very little respect from others for drudgery. Drudgery has little in it to be proud of. So when a teen asks *"Why should I do this?"* it may be the beginning of an argument, but it also signals his need for appreciation for doing the job. He's counting on your support for activities that are not very important, fun, or "adult." His question about drudgery is a signal to focus on encouraging him and praising him for a job well done. Also, you may need concrete rewards as in the token economies described in Step 4.

Learning Must Be Useful Now

Parents must provide experiences that point out, here and now, the usefulness of things learned in school. Certainly even a ten- or twelve-year-old can handle a checking account for the family, or plan and carry out the family food shopping. For school subjects that do not easily apply to daily tasks, parents can influence their teen's respect for the subject by asking questions.

> Mom: *"What was your work in science today?"*
> Greg: *"We numbered the chambers of the heart and followed a drop of blood through the system."*
> Mom: *"I always wanted to know more about that. How does it go through?"*

Show interest in school projects and point out, from news-of-the-day, where knowledge applies. Parent-teen conversations that bring in schoolwork show the usefulness of Greg's work and improve his respect for himself.

A Crucial Growing-Up Question: "How Can I Make the Grade?"
(Homework Strategies that Work)

Greg's second complaint about school also showed up in Geography. **This time it wasn't that he questioned the usefulness of the subject by saying it's "boring," but that he found it "boring" because he was not doing well.** This requires parental help beyond showing the topic's usefulness—Greg needs study skills.

Homework that requires staring at materials and memorization can be boring and hard to stick with:

> Greg: *"I just can't keep the states straight. We're supposed to know them by next Friday!"*
> Dad: *"What are they going to ask you about them?"*
> Greg: *"We have to point them out on a blank map with no words or anything."*
> Dad: *"Do you have a map?"*

> Greg: *"I have the one in this book. I've been studying it a lot, but I don't remember much."*
>
> Dad: *"How do you do the "studying" part?"*
>
> Greg: *"Well, I look at the states and try to remember which ones go where."*
>
> Dad: *"Greg, I think you need to go through a few drills in a situation like the one you're going to have next Friday. How about tracing that map so we can have one that's blank like the one you'll see on Friday. Then we'll make a few copies when we go shopping."*
>
> Greg: *OK. Then I could practice by filling in the names on the copies we make."*

Studying requires practice. Greg has been trying to practice in his mind *("I've been studying it a lot")*, but sitting and staring at a book or homework sheet is not real practice—performance—and Greg has not made much progress.

To make homework time successful, Dad first asks Greg what he is *doing*. **Most students who are falling behind don't have a specific target for their effort.** When they study, they stare at things—notes or books—they don't *DO* anything.

Most of us don't have the kind of memory that retains a great deal from just looking; it's the *doing* that will be remembered.

What do you remember from your high school days? Spelling? Math and vocabulary you still use (*do* things with)? But I'll bet you remember very little of social studies, geography, history, or math you never use.

We usually tell our teens to *"work hard"* in school. The "work hard" idea is good advice but by itself leaves out the specifics. **Successful work shows up in grades if the student is shown** how the "work hard" idea is turned into overt practice; not just staring at pages, but reading aloud; not just "trying to remember," but talking to others about the work; drilling important concepts, rewriting notes and important material, and drawing new diagrams or tables that organize facts differently. That's how the idea of "work hard" becomes successful learning.

If you are skeptical of this strategy, try the following experiment:

> *Pick out a favorite magazine in which there are two articles or stories you have not yet read. Read the first story to yourself in your usual way. Find someone to listen to your report of the story or article and tell them all the detail you can remember —who wrote it, who was in it, what was going on, conclusions reached and so on.*
>
> *Now go back to the magazine and read the second article or story. This time, stand up and read out loud, with good emphasis and inflection— to the wall if necessary. Now find your listener again and report this story giving all the details you can remember of who, what, and where.*

By the end of the second report, you will notice how much more you remember of the second story. As one student put it to me, *"Well of course I remember that one, I remember what I said!"*

For the purpose of learning and changing habits there is no substitute for active practice. **On your vacation, stare at pages in a novel while lying on the beach if you enjoy it, but if it's for learning, "work hard."**

Reading assignments often lead the student to this mistake of leaving out the *doing* part of learning. Many of my students have said, *"I can't believe I did poorly. I went through (stared at) all the material for the test!"*

If you only read it (not really practice) and never use it, it will be gone soon. If reading is the assignment, have your student take reading notes—preferably on cards—for each page. *"Never turn a page without writing something,"* should be the rule.

Giving Your Student the Advantage

The reading-note requirement has several advantages.

1. Notes become a source of motivation because they are a concrete product which can give the student a feeling of accomplishment.

2. Notes are a product that the parent can encourage, review, and use as a basis for other rewards, if that's in the plan.

3. The third and most important advantage is that notes provide benchmarks of progress that allow the student to pick up at the right place after an interruption.

   It's surprising how much studying is done in small sessions of only a few minutes between interruptions by phone calls, snacks, and chores. Without a note-taking habit, most of us start again at the same place we started before. With past notes, we have a record of where we are and can move on to new material.

4. At review time, the work is condensed as notes, maps, tables, and drill sheets guaranteeing the right material will be memorized. Your student can thereby avoid the misery of thrashing madly through unorganized papers.

How About a Computer Program
to Help Learning?

Computer programs from school or at home can be helpful, especially if the drills are very similar to the other school work and to the tests that evaluate progress. Math and language programs often include useful drills because the content of the drills and the test that comes up later are almost exactly the same.

But for programs in other areas where content can vary, you'll need advice from school about *what* spelling, history, government, or social studies the program should cover.

B. F. Skinner, the behavioral psychologist, said computer programs (he called them "teaching machines" in the 1960's) would take over most of the activity in the future schoolrooms of the 1980's and beyond. His prediction was right in that the programs have become a part of many classrooms and libraries, but their application is far short of Skinner's expectations. What happened?

Skinner felt that success with questions and answers would be enough incentive to keep the student working. But for most children, the novelty of working the screen wears off, and adult encouragements and real life applications are needed to keep interest up. It's the same support from parents and teachers that homework and lessons have always required. **Leaving a student on a chair, even one in front of a computer, may not produce learning that shows up on school tests unless parents provide encouragement to keep the practice going.**

A second limitation of computer effectiveness is in the *action* **the student is asked to perform.** Remember, learning is in the *doing*. If a student learns to press the right buttons on a keyboard to answer math questions, his performance will be best there and not as good on paper and pencil tests and verbal drills.

It's amazing to us adults that learning 3 plus 5 or the usefulness of 3.1416 on a computer doesn't result in a correct answer on that point on every test paper after that. The student can improve with a computer program, but **how the improvement shows up on tests depends on how similar the test is to the program, not only in content, but in the _way_ the student is asked to provide answers.**

Here's another place you can contribute: make up some tests. Arrange to collect information from your teen's school. You need to know the nature and general format of the evaluations they use in the computer subjects you will have at home. Then, you can construct practice tests on the computer material, but in the format and style your student will encounter at school. Perhaps *your student* could make up these practice tests for himself and others. Quizzes and drills with pencil and paper will give your teen practice in expressing the answers as required later—when no keyboard is around.

An Additional Schoolroom Strategy

Counselors often coach students to improve their *classroom* habits as well as study habits. Use incentives to encourage your teen to try them also, particularly in classes where your student is "having trouble with the teacher."

1. **A student influences a teacher's attitude just as a teacher influences a student's:** When there is a choice, your student could sit in a seat as close to the front as possible and keep good eye contact with the teacher during presentations—just as you would practice good listening skills in a private situation.

2. **Your student should be alert for a question to ask concerning the material.** A continual banter of questions that are unnecessary will do no good, but good questions help learning _and_ teaching. **Einstein's mother used to ask him when he came home from school,** _"Did you ask any good questions today?"_ If you try to ask good questions in class, you have reasons to follow the teacher's presentations more closely, and are more likely to learn.

3. **Your student should occasionally talk to the teacher about the subject.** On at least a weekly basis, he should speak to the teacher about the class with a question or comparison to some aspect of other subjects or experiences.

Some people may object to the contrived nature of these suggestions, but **many teens have the mistaken notion that the classroom is, or should be, a place where completely passive learning takes place.**

The student needs to know that an active, assertive role is necessary. The fact is that a classroom is a social situation where exchanges are a part of the learning. The exchanges may not influence the teacher's grading, but your teen's relationship with his/her teacher will improve active learning and _that_ will improve grades!

Guidelines for Homework Time

A Harvard professor I know always distributes a slip of paper to each student before class. The top line on the slip reads, _"The main point of the day was . . ."_ followed by a space for the student to complete the statement. The next line says, _"My question for_ *today is...* " followed by more writing room.

The professor collects the slips each day to see how the main point has been understood and what confusion is in need of more attention during the next class. Students must think, summarize, and question, and the professor has excellent feedback. Many professors now use this procedure.

Even before your teen goes to Harvard, the question-and-answer game can help with school work. Try this exercise in question-asking practice:

Explain that you are going to play a question and information game related to the media and school.

1. The parent picks a science news program or written article heard or seen lately and makes up a question about the information. For example, *"This morning I read an article about the eclipse today. What I want to know is, why is the moon just the right size to cover our view of the sun?"*

    Answering each question is not necessary, but if this happens, it's a plus to the main goal of the game, which is to focus on the usefulness of each subject or media item.

2. Now, it's the teen's turn to ask a question about school subject material. Choose classes in which learning needs to be improved. For example, *"Can you point to a place on the map where four states come together?"* Repeat the game occasionally with different subjects.

3. A follow-up to the game is for the teen to ask questions in classes at school. Compliment your teen for questions and encourage discussion about the information. If your teen didn't ask a question, have him/her write the ones that would have been best to ask.

The more activity (forming questions and taking notes) your student does with the study material, the more real learning he or she will accomplish. Evaluate these study methods and encourage your child to use the ones that work best for him or her.

The most important advice on learning comes from early history when Sophocles said, *"The learning is in the doing of the thing."* If you wanted to improve your tennis, you would

> *Learning is in the doing.*

probably arrange time to practice on the courts. If you wanted to learn new guitar strums, you would practice them. When it comes to school work, it's easy for the student to forget how much *practice counts*.

The following guidelines summarize the important points for homework time.

GUIDELINE 1
Use Homework Time in an Active Way!

Action Example 1: Always have pencil and paper handy when reading. Note-taking is good practice, and good practice is good learning. Take notes on every page of reading. **Authors and publishers of school books are always struggling to keep the size and expense of books down; every page has something to say. What is it? Write it down.**

It's a good idea to put many of these notes in question form. The student should use the headings in the book to make up the questions and use note cards if they are convenient. Note cards encourage review of specifics. **As test-time approaches, students with the note-taking habit will already have their own review to study!**

Action Example 2: Students should make new lists, drawings and
summaries of class materials. **Any new "doing" will help the
student remember.** Working with other students can produce
the same kind of practice and drill. New lists, drawings and
charts are more easily remembered by those who create them. **I
have never had a student fail a course when he produced
study notes and other evidence of practice!**

Action Example 3: Make up the test. If your students are still
concerned about a test, they should construct their own version
of the test trying to make it as similar to the one expected.
Students often report that more than half of their questions were
the same as the ones on the teacher's test! With those questions
answered in advance, the students easily remembered their
answers and were quickly half way to a good test grade.

Action Example 4: Keep a calendar! The calendar should include
plans for homework for each day and a record of successes. It
should also include priorities for assignments to study so time is
spent on the most important work of the moment.

GUIDELINE 2
Reinforce Practice

Many competing activities have built-in payoffs, but the benefits of studying are often a long way off. Stanley Student becomes
more efficient as good study skills develop. It is not a dramatic
change, it's just that the longer you practice good habits the more
reliable and useful they become. This includes study habits: taking
study notes, re-doing materials, and keeping a calendar. Future
opportunities, grades and preparation for new subjects will have
long-range benefits but are weak motivators for present effort.

So what can a teacher or parent do to reinforce a student who needs to acquire new attitudes and skills to study effectively?

While the calendar helps in planning time to study, parents need to help in planning a place to study.

1. Provide a place where active note-taking is convenient. This is just as important to the learning place as freedom from distraction.

2. Talk about subjects the students are taking and create examples of the usefulness of the material.

3. Reinforce knowledge about the subjects by asking questions—even questions that stump the parents as well as the student and make it necessary to look up the answer in the homework materials.

4. Reinforce and praise *daily and weekly grades* that reflect knowledge learned.

GUIDELINE 3
Use a Strategy for Tests

Even after students have acquired good study habits through the guidelines of their own practice and encouragement from parents and teachers, they often complain about having trouble with tests. These test strategies bring positive results in either essay or objective tests.

During objective tests: Certainly every student intends to answer each question, but very often items go unanswered. Two reasons for this are: fear of guessing and failure to remember the question. The student should carefully read *and eliminate* options. Checking off poor choices allows the student to focus on the remaining options and improve chances that small differences will be discovered. Once an answer is selected, the student should read the first part of the item one more time to be sure that the selection actually answers this particular question. Wrong options are often, in themselves, correct, but not the answer to the initial question.

For essay tests: The important guideline here is to answer each question twice—once in outline form and then as an essay answer. The student should write a brief outline on another sheet before beginning essay answers. This first answer can be in the student's own words and shorthand. For example, in response to the question, *"What was important about the Gettysburg Address?"* the student might jot down, *"Lincoln; at graveyard; during Civil War; trying to unite the country; said country must try hard to finish the war; for equality and people to run government; give quote."*

Now, looking at the first answer, the student is likely to complete the second answer in good form. Also, as the student is writing the final answer, new points may come to mind to add to the final answer. The teacher is more likely to give a high score when the major points are easy to find. And major points will be found more easily if your student's writing is as neat as possible. If this is a problem, buy an erasable ink pen before the next test!

Learning is a Required Activity of Life

Students often believe that if only they could get through school, the demands of learning would be over. Adults know that new learning tasks are always presenting themselves both on the job and at home.

Many of the specifics of school lessons will be forgotten, but the means for finding and learning them again will prepare your child for most challenges. Students with good learning habits will always have an easier and more enjoyable experience with each new opportunity in both their work and home life.

SOCIAL SKILLS

"How Can I Get the Kids to Like Me?"

After *"Mom, can we talk?"* and *"How can I make good grades?"* another crucial growing-up question is, *"Mom, how can I get other kids to like me?"*

What a heart-breaking question! Remember Greg had this problem as part of his trouble with school. Of course there are no quick-fix answers, but a parent can pass along rules of conversation and a little advice about being interested in the other person.

> Brian: *"So, Greg, how did your soccer game go?"*
> Greg: *"What? Oh, it was OK."*
> Brian: *"Must have been a mess with all that rain."*
> Greg: *"Yeah, you should have seen the mud down at the goal; our goalie looked like a pig!"*
> Brian: *"Our field still had some grass down there."*
> Greg: *"Did you have to play that Kickers team?"*
> Brian: *"Yes. Have you played them already?"*

Brian has a good social habit of an occasional question. Most adults learn early that part of getting along is remembering to express some genuine unselfish interest and *liking* for others.

Teens can be cynical and believe that being "likable" is "inborn" and each of us must suffer with our inherited "personality." But most adults have seen a low responder like Greg "brighten up" or "turn around" with a compliment or question that shows interest in his life. How responsive and "attractive" Greg is can change. It depends on his companions *and his own effort.*

Brian's attractive habit is often imitated and Greg, not usually outgoing, picks up the topic and finally has a question of his own about "that Kickers team." Brian partly creates his own pleasant social world. Both Brian and Greg probably like each other because of the reactions they "draw out" of each other.

Being "Likable" is More than Asking Questions

So some kids are likable for reasons way beyond appearance and "personality." We parents know that being "likable" is also made up of specific behaviors; it's a matter of *showing* some genuine unselfish *liking* of others. People with this attractive habit are not only likable but also are often imitated. Therefore, they create more attractive behavior in the people around them.

Just asking a few questions, as Brian does, will not turn a person's social life around. He will need to make other efforts as well. And he may still believe that appearance is first on the *"Likable Characteristics List"* and that saying clever, cool, or funny remarks is second.

> *Being "likable" is a matter of showing some genuine unselfish liking of others.*

The characteristic missing from the list usually shows up when our teen is asked who *he* likes. Usually, the answer is that he likes people who accept him, admire him, and want to spend time with *him*!

Sometimes the view from the other person's perspective leads to the discovery that: *"To be liked, I should watch out for being too critical and make an effort in my social habits."* This would include habits of asking about the other person but would add showing concern, complimenting, expressing agreement instead of criticism, and paying attention to the five conversational rules given in Step 1.

One mom described the difference between her daughters to me this way: *"Dianne and her sister Kelly are so different! Kelly can't stop talking and Dianne hardly says a word. It's hard to believe they were raised in the same family!*

"Last week, I picked them up from a neighborhood party and when I asked them how it went, Kelly said, 'It was great! They dropped all these balloons on us and everyone screamed! Sally was there, Ann was there, Betty, Millie, and all the boys, Frank, Donald, David and Cris.'"

When Mom asked Dianne how it went she just said, *"It was OK. Everyone was running all over."* But Kelly said Dianne just stood around.

Being sociable is like many other activities: If you're good at it, you like it, and you tend to practice more of it. On the other hand, if you don't get started with others easily, then you will have a little less practice and the circle continues.

Kelly's focus is on others; she asks a lot of questions and remembers a lot of details about others that she is forever talking about. Dianne's concern is for her own security. She can't seem to think of anything safe to say.

Both girls have habits that perpetuate their attitudes. Kelly talks a great deal, she is loud, and she has learned about the other kids. Dianne doesn't talk much, she uses a soft voice, and her lack of experience with the others leaves her short on subjects to bring up.

Dianne doesn't have a "problem." She has a quiet style which sometimes makes her feel left out, but she shouldn't be given the extra burden of being told she has something wrong with her.

Her parents could give her extra social ammunition before she goes into a social situation. Adults help each other with this kind of priming quite often: *"Remember* (Mom says on the way to her office party with Dad) *my boss, Jane, has a boat out on the town lake, and she just got back from Florida. Tom bought a car like ours, and Bob Teak's daughter recently made him a grandfather."*

These little bits of information will allow Dad to *"go more than half way"* in starting some conversation with Mom's co-workers—if he wants to.

Dianne needs some help with information too. She may complain that *"No one came over to me at the party,"* but the parental reflex of *"Did you go over to any of them?"* could be left off while providing whatever information might be helpful to Dianne in thinking up something to start a conversation.

Dad doesn't get a lecture on how to correct some defect in himself on the way to Mom's party, he's just provided with a better chance of doing what he wants to do with information about the others. And Dianne doesn't need more criticism either, just some long-term help as the situations come up so that if she is inclined to join in the talk, the detail of thinking of a topic will be easier.

> *In order to be likable, teens will have to do some liking.*

A person who is good at socializing has many friends; they laugh at the same things and cooperate on the same tasks. They don't seem to try to please each other, they just do. The notion of being pleasing in order to get along with others may seem a little simple-minded and of little use until pleasing, agreeing, disagreeing, fighting and cooperating are seen as special cases of social rewards and punishments.

Most teens worry about how attractive or likable they are and certainly some primping before an outing can make a difference. However, like adults, *they* think their attractiveness is largely based on their physical appearance while their judgment of others largely depends on what the others *do*! So it follows that in order to be lik*able*, teens will have to do some lik*ing*.

Cool, moody, critical, sarcastic, angry, or bitter people make interesting characters in movies. But in real life, such characters are not well-liked because they rarely show that they like others!

Without making an effort to like others, teens may have uneasy and insecure feelings. At the end of an evening with peers they probably feel they missed something. *Liking is a behavior that bears a message to the receiver*, a communication that must be sent in order to be received. Consider the following example.

Anne was nervous before John came by for her. When all her adjusting and posturing in front of the mirror was done, the best help would be to plan ways to show she liked John. Physical attractiveness is important, but the other part of being attractive is letting your friend or date know you like him or her. Anne adjusted her hair after the walk to the car and remembered not to slouch when they were riding along. She wondered if he would like her to talk about his football game.

> *Liking is a behavior that bears a message to the receiver, a communication that must be sent in order to be received.*

Did Anne look at the date from John's side? If she did, she needed to show it by asking John some questions about his activities, family, job, and school work. She probably needs to do some planning of these topics before the next date. If she did like John, she didn't show it because she was too preoccupied with herself.

Did John think Anne liked him? He didn't know, so he fell into the same mistake Anne was trying to avoid in the first place—worrying about being lik*able* when a little lik*ing* would have been a better strategy. He wondered how he could impress Anne: Tell her about the football game? Drive in a daring way? Tell her about his latest success? Instead, he should have *sent his own liking messages—asking questions about Anne and complimenting her.*

Would Anne go out with him again? Maybe—if she liked him *and* if she thought she was liked! Will he call again? Anne probably thought that depended on whether he liked her or not. Partly. But it also depended on whether he thought he was liked.

Liking and Caring Behaviors are Attractive

Do your family members use liking behaviors? If so, then preparing for an outing will not be a stressful time for your teen because he/she understands the basics that make a person likable. The moments before a party can be planning time: *"At the party I want to spend time with . . . I want to talk to . . . I will show I like those persons by . . ."*

Natural liking behaviors are consistent attention, questions, encouragement, and praise, instead of preoccupation with your own looks and interests. If you do more asking and listening than you do telling, then you're probably on the right track. Liking behaviors are habits that grow with practice and replace their opposites—criticism, sarcasm, and negative comments.

Answers are impressive, but questions send the messages. A teen asks about her boyfriend's studying; he asks about her day. The messages show concern—they say, *"I'm interested in you."*

In marital counseling a common assignment for both members of the couple is to have "caring days"—days when he or she does a particular thing for his or her spouse— without being asked or expecting anything in return. What do you suppose is the request most often listed for the caring day by the wife? She says, *"I wish he would ask me about* **my** *day."* Out of all the things a husband could do, this simple wish is the most common request: personalized interest and attention.

> *Liking behaviors are habits that grow with practice and replace their opposites—criticism, sarcasm, and negative comments.*

Liking is not always returned, and two-way relationships never balance exactly. One person is always required to go more than half-way to make it work. Socially successful and likable people put out more than their share of effort in relationships that are not ideally balanced in regard to effort.

Teens need to live with less than ideal situations at times, and discover when to accept and when to change a relationship, so as not to be unfairly used. Keeping too tight a score on how much you put yourself out for someone may keep things so even that the relationship is not appreciated. *"Having a little in the bank"* with persons at home or school can help smooth troubles as they come up with those people.

When talking with your teen about why certain people are attractive, look at the behaviors of those people. Teens need to discover that Richard Dreyfuss and Kathleen Turner are attractive for a combination of reasons. Their physical characteristics are not easily copied, but look carefully at how Richard Dreyfuss plays in his romantic scenes. He's concerned, involved, and ready to be a part of his leading lady's solution to problems. John Travolta danced through *Saturday Night Fever* staring into the eyes of his leading lady.

Isn't this the fantasy, *"If he were here, he would be interested in me, too?"* **When a film wishes to portray the disillusionment of the common fellow who pursues a beautiful and too-sophisticated woman, the script doesn't turn her ugly—just vain, uninterested and not capable of liking others.**

The Media Aids Communication About Social Skills

Parents can use the popularity of the media with teenagers to trigger listening times. When teens and parents watch a TV show together or read the same magazine article, they can talk it over. Ask teens about the situations or characters' actions. Raise questions and then listen, instead of moralizing. Listening helps teens express their developing views; telling them what to think turns them off to the adult and the topic.

Teens and parents need variety from the daily routine and repetitious discussion topics: friends, school, and hobbies. When Mom and Dad make separate lists of topics they discuss with their teenager, TV programs often show up on the list. Parents may see TV as an intruder to parental influence, but it is a rich source of neutral, lively subjects for conversation, especially when adults and teens watch together.

> Dad: *"What did you think of that show?"*
> Lisa: *"The babies stole the audience! They were cute."*
> Dad: *"Never cried or needed diaper changes."*
> Lisa: *"Not very realistic, I guess, but I liked the way the grandpa talked to the twins."*
> Dad: *"Babies need to hear a lot of talk to learn."*

TV situations are not threatening because they happen to someone else and the teen has as much information as the parent since both watched the same show. Help your teens react to and question TV shows, instead of simply letting them be passive viewers. You have your attitudes and answers to life's questions, and TV can help your teens form their views, especially when someone is there to listen and ask questions.

How the media portray sexuality is a good example. TV and magazines sell products by using material about sex to attract and keep audiences. They show sex in favorable ways, while omitting negatives. Casual and irresponsible sex looks like innocent fun on TV, but we are not shown the realistic side: the stress and need for understanding and intimacy on many levels. We are often spared any discussion of unwanted pregnancy, abortion, and the nine-month stresses of pregnancy without a husband's support. Television rarely shows someone caring for a sick baby, an AIDS patient, or a victim of venereal disease.

In a short time span the media cannot possibly cover the 18 years it takes to raise a person from baby to adult, or the lifetime commitment of being a parent. Parents who discuss media's omissions with their teens can raise questions about these issues occasionally and provide a means to help teens develop their own adjustment to sexuality.

A Disposition Creates Its Own Surroundings

When kids imitate bad dispositions, they must use threats in a subtle way because they are less powerful than adults. Fighting back, a teen puts off her parents or teacher and reduces their requests for work. That reaction creates further negative reactions from adults who are viewed by the teen as confirmation of her cynical expectations of others.

Consider Lisa at age 14. She has developed a negative attitude and is often cynical and pessimistic at school. You can imagine that it is easy to feel uncomfortable or aggravated around her. At home with her family, Lisa receives a bit more attention, but the aggravation and frustration that others feel usually shows through:

> Mom: *"How was school today, Lisa?"*
> Lisa: *"OK."*
> Mom: *"Well, tell me about it!"*
> Lisa: *"Do you have to know everything?"*
> Mom: *"I was just interested."*
> Lisa: *"Just leave me alone."*

Lisa is a non-rewarder. She is self-centered, thinking little of others and asking little of them. She's no trouble, but somehow she's still troublesome. She brings out the worst in others and then reacts to that by getting worse herself. The cycle continues. **To break the cycle, someone will have to be big enough to not play the game. That requires love, because it means performing good social behavior with no support from Lisa, possibly with punishment from her instead.**

Lisa herself might grow up enough to be the "someone" who will break the cycle someday. However, in the short run, it's not likely that anyone will spontaneously change. The most likely adjustment Lisa will make is to *"give them back what they give you."* If they give you bad behavior, let them taste their own medicine! Punishment for punishment; silence for silence, or even, silence for punishment *("They won't get anything out of me!").*

Lisa may extend her use of punishment and later, learn to use warnings of punishments to coerce teacher or parent. If demands are not met, she increases the intensity of the demand, and then she uses nastiness or possibly a tantrum. It's coercion.

Adults may learn to avoid all this punishment by giving in early. Giving in serves as reward to Lisa, but it also rewards the adults because they successfully avoid Lisa's escalating nastiness. **It is a common parent-child relationship where** *the child's bad behavior is rewarded* **by getting undeserved privileges and avoiding work, and** *the parent's "giving in" is rewarded* **by successfully avoiding the threat of more bad behavior.** It's a case of negative reinforcement (see Step 7) for parents and positive reinforcement for Lisa.

In order to have an effect on Lisa, the adults around her will need to model and maintain a more positive disposition than Lisa does.

Teenagers and Parents Learn Each Other's Habits

A teen's most common reaction to everyday problems will probably be to imitate people he or she lives with at home and in school. Children becoming teens imitate *styles* of adults more often than specific adult behaviors.

Attitudes toward others, conversational style and temperament are the durable characteristics of teachers and parents that are copied. The result is a general disposition made up of habits and styles of encouragement and punishment of others. **A teen can easily acquire a disposition almost entirely from the family air!**

The disposition to punish and correct others can be learned just as easily as the disposition to encourage others. But to learn to police your disposition is a difficult task. There are no planned consequences for *you* as an adult, and adults change by practice with encouragements just as children do. So whether or not anything can be done about the dispositions in your home depends on the answer to the question *"Can these parents control themselves through conscientious effort and through feedback from their partner?"*

The positive approach emphasizes reward—not necessarily material ones, but approval, praise, smiling, etc. The job becomes a more pleasant one for you as a parent and leaves you with a child who is still informative, friendly, responsive, and not always wanting to go somewhere else!

The choice between rewards and punishments that make up a disposition will be taken up in detail in Steps 7 and 8, but in most cases the odds favor reward. **Punishment shows that out of all the responses your teen could have made, he has chosen the wrong one—try again. Little information is available in that.**

A positive reaction is much more efficient because it says that out of all the things he could have done, this is one of the right ones. A rewarding reaction is more difficult for parents, however, because they must take time to decide what they want to reward and what comment or material thing to use as reward. **We're more likely to already know what we want to punish and how we would do it.**

If you are a single parent, it may be all the more difficult to say to yourself, as a spouse might: *"Don't let me pick on the kids; stop me and point out my good reactions."* Step 10 takes up this and other problems of going it alone.

The family's disposition can also be influenced by making plans about the small everyday social behaviors of kids. Many parents have developed a poor disposition in their child by not planning the limits of *their* demands as carefully as they plan the kids' limits. A teen makes *so* many mistakes, we want him to do *so* many things right, and he can do *so* many things wrong. Without a plan, the parents aren't sure what is right and what is wrong or where the limits are, so they are constantly after the kids for this behavior or that one.

Amazing Copies!

"Isn't it amazing how mother and daughter are alike!" said Ms. Jones. *"That woman reading at the end of the back row just <u>has</u> to be Regina's mother. Regina even reads at lunch time!"*

"Yes, it's unbelievable," whispered Ms. Miller. *"And I would recognize Bobby Comic's father anywhere. His attempt at a little joke. And Lisa Sour's father sulking while he waits for the meeting. You wouldn't believe such details could be inherited!"*

Ms. Jones and Ms. Miller are teachers at PTA back-to-school night. They told me that when they were waiting for the meeting to start, they played a "Match the Parents Game." It's been their favorite for years and they find their guesses to be very accurate.

Their success with matching parents and students comes, in part, from physical similarities that are inherited, but the way the students act is partly a copy of their parents' styles. It's a hint the teachers find very useful in their game. How talkative, pleasant, sarcastic, or happy each parent and student is, helps the teachers make their matches and they are very successful.

Everyone contributes to the family atmosphere. Each contributor also follows the lead of the others—modeling, imitating, and reacting in a manner appropriate to past experience. Respectful, loving parental reactions are copied by the children in their responses back to the parents and to others. The social habits of the children and the parents recycle through the family, creating the general atmosphere as these habits are repeated.

STEP 4
Make Room for Your Teen to Be Useful *and* to be "Weird"

The school, social, and domestic skills your teen learns need to be put to use right away. The more they know, the more likely they are to take up the activities of a full life, and the self-esteem they experience from being useful will provide some of the protection they'll need when they encounter the dangerous temptations discussed in Step 5.

BEING USEFUL
Coach Teens to Find Life's Adventures and Fun

Everyone seeks variety in life, but teens seem to require heavy doses just to feel good about themselves and to keep from falling into depression. *"Do you have to do something every night? Why is continual entertainment necessary? Can't teens just sit down and relax for a while?"* parents may ask.

TV and movies give teens romantic notions of all the adventure and excitement that might be passing them by. Teens want a lot of action. They have already developed many adult capabilities and have an amazing amount of energy available. They also have a lot of ideas about the opportunities out there. Instead of satisfaction from everyday events, they seek dramatic happenings to fulfill their need for action.

Adults have discovered the mild satisfaction of doing everyday activities: job accomplishments, house and yard work, bills and taxes to pay, shopping for a new TV, book, or gadget. These chores are not the adventurous activities a teenager has in mind, but they do provide a need we all have for worthwhile actions.

Activities and Chores Offer Satisfaction

The teen's need to "do something" is usually not specific and needs some adult direction. Having several things you want to do helps you get through a slow day or week. Activities don't need to be tennis, skiing, movies, or going out with the gang; they can be puttering, shopping, or fixing things. These alternatives usually don't start out as fun, but they do get rid of the blues.

> *Chores don't start out as fun, but they do get rid of the blues.*

Obsessions with music, video games, or TV may play a useful role in the teen's appetite for excitement in a world with limited opportunities for him or her. They may also be symptoms of needs for expanded personal responsibilities that give personal pride.

Fourteen-year-old Maya had a big day coming up: she would turn in the social studies project she had worked on for a week and give a short talk about her science project. The band was meeting, and she would play her trumpet. After school she had to shop for shoes and help make supper. Later she and Dad were going to change the oil on the car. Nothing very adventurous, but a schedule of activities she felt good about.

Thirteen-year-old Brent was thinking over his day at school and afterwards: he expected flack for his late reading report, and math was confusing because he had skipped the homework for two nights. Even when he was not in trouble at school he had a hard time focusing on his work. After school, his friends were practicing football while he was ineligible until he raised his grades. His hobbies, biking and mixing music, were on hold until he fixed his bike and radio. At a peak of

> *There's nothing more dangerous than human beings with too much time on their hands.*

energy in his life, Brent needs adult help with repairs and incentives to do his schoolwork and chores.

There's nothing more dangerous than human beings with too much time on their hands. All kings, army officers, college presidents, and teachers learn this principle early or suffer the consequences. So again, planning incentives for productive activity is needed because if some structuring is not provided for a teen at loose ends, over the undirected years he or she will come up with some undesirable habits. Teens may entertain themselves in very bothersome ways if they have no responsibilities to fulfill, no opportunities for useful activity, and no reason to expect any benefit from their choices.

The constant watching here is for a teen's opportunities. It's not necessary to see that she always has something to do. Everyone needs a break and has their own pace of living. But on-going responsibilities provide something to do, something to be proud of and something that is a source of self-esteem.

Help Teens Focus on Schoolwork and Chores

When you first suggest an activity to a teenager, you may meet objections. That's when it's time to think of incentives to get things going. A teen needs help to start adult chores and focus on important activities such as schoolwork and fulfilling hobbies. Without some direction, you can expect complaining and escape to less worthwhile time fillers, such as TV. Possibly your companionship in the chore would help: do the dishes with me, not for me; work in the yard with me, and shop for groceries with me.

> *Without some direction, you can expect complaining and escape to less worthwhile time fillers, such as TV.*

Brent's homework and project problems will only be solved by trying numerous alternatives. We adults have learned the activities we like, and we enjoy the therapeutic effects. How can Brent's mother pass along these insights? Brent's reaction to her suggestions is not likely to be encouraging, and Mom will have to continue to help without much appreciation from him. Frequent positive feedback for small successes *here* and *now* will help Brent try alternatives and practice important skills.

"Brent, if you show me your completed math and science work, you can go to the ice rink with Roger." Mom had seen so much trouble with Brent and his schoolwork before that now she insists he *earn* privileges. After her complaints, he always argued, *"When I leave middle school I will do a lot better!"* Not satisfied with promises in the far-off future, Mom insisted that his incentives come as a result of his efforts, not just as freebies.

Mom checks frequently with Brent's teachers to ensure that his work is up-to-date. Brent responded to the incentives, and they helped him focus on important behaviors and earn a feeling of pride for his efforts.

Practice, Man, Practice

Many jokesters know the old one about the visitor who stopped a native New Yorker and asked how to get to Carnegie Hall. The New Yorker answered, *"Practice, man, practice!"*

When practice has been lacking, painful experiences are ahead for a teen about to leave the nest. Life has disadvantages awaiting a girl with little experience deciding what to eat, when to eat, what to wear and when to wear it, what to say when making a dental appointment, and how to distinguish between "free" and "on credit"—a distinction lost on many credit card holders now in trouble.

Without practice in all of these skills in her teenage years she will feel a little inadequate, dependent, and may question her own worth. As she leaves the family's protection, she will need to learn fast in a situation that is not as loving as the family, and she will bring little confidence to the task. **Growing up, that is, practicing to be an adult, requires a lot of parent-planned practice.**

As the girl or boy who is unpracticed leaves for college or work or both, his or her parents will blurt out a last-minute barrage of instructions. Whether practice was left out because it seemed

> *When practice has been lacking, painful experiences are ahead for a teen about to leave the nest.*

to risk too many mistakes, take too much time in the frantic family activities, or was withheld for protection's sake, in the end, parents realize there are consequences to reap and now they rush to get in all those cautions: *"Be sure you brush your teeth, get your rest, open a checking account, and choose friends wisely!"*

The first experience of being away from home can be all the more difficult and lonely if our offspring-now-sprung has little confidence in deciding when to study and when to rest, because parents always settled those questions before.

Many of my college students go to a campus counselor with the complaint that no one seems to care about them at the big university. A great deal of the "care" the student misses should have been gradually withdrawn years ago to make room for practice and pride in self. **The only place there is love enough for all that practice is in the family.**

> *The only place there is love enough for all that practice is in the family.*

One of my students complained about doing his own laundry because he didn't understand all those selections of cycles and what to wash with what. He was embarrassed to say all his underwear were now pink! I joked that he could throw away his dirty socks and underwear and buy new ones. Taking me seriously, he cried, *"I don't know my size!"* For 19 years the little number on the back elastic of his underwear followed him around along with other little notes on washing instructions, but he had no need of them as long as Mom was there. But now she wasn't.

Almost all of my students manage to survive the passage from home to campus despite painful evenings learning their size and how to use a washing machine. So lack of practice didn't cause a great deal of permanent damage.

But in many cases, a critical period of childhood that could have nurtured a feeling of self-worth and comfort with life was missed. Later, *complete* development of self-confidence may be difficult or impossible to secure.

Practice Makes Almost Perfect

All of us can remember the idea of practice in school work and we understand the necessity for practice when teaching something new. But when we are not teaching such things as tying shoelaces, playing the piano, or learning to drive a car, we often forget the importance of practice. It applies just as well to bed-making, dish-washing, time management and how to get along with others.

If you, as parent, do these jobs for your teen, he or she gets no practice. It is easy to be overprotective and slow down learning: *"I'll take your library book back," "I'll get your running shoes repaired," "I'll be your time manager, you just do what I say,"* and, *"I'll call for your dental appointment—you wait."*

> *It is easy to be overprotective and slow down learning.*

Some parents will protest that if they let their teen do these things, mistakes will happen. She'll be fined for late library books, never get the shoes fixed, waste time until deadlines pass, or say the wrong thing on the phone. All true. And each parent will have to make the judgment—is she or he ready? Not, *"Is she ready to be perfect?"* But, *"Is he ready to gain <u>something</u> from practice?"* We shouldn't wait until a teen is ready to do it *without a flaw*. That may take forever.

Another advantage to early practice is that your child-teen can gain much to be proud of *now*. It's true you can't rely on a 13-year-old to pick a perfect diet, yet even 35-year-olds don't have perfect diets either. But you do need to give over responsibilities so that you can guarantee your opportunities to encourage your teen's progress. A wise parent creates practice, not just for learning, but to improve a teen's *self-respect* and confidence.

Practice and Reward

Perhaps you found that, in learning to play a musical instrument, even practice was not enough. And yet practice was enough to perfect your handwriting. **What are the differences between your brief piano experience and your "learned forever" handwriting?**

In learning to improve your handwriting, you were rewarded not only for the hours of practice but also for the first little successes. You wrote your own name, a friend's name, then a note to a friend and a letter to grandpa. The improvements were useful, shared with others, and practice continued.

But too often the first improvements in playing the scale on the piano produce little or no admiration, they seem of little use, and are a long way from the performance dreamed of. Sometimes piano lessons are successful because learning a favorite piece or popular song was part of the early training. If that consideration was a part of your music lessons, practice probably

> *What are the differences between your brief piano experience and your "learned forever" handwriting?*

continued. If not, you may have quit, but I bet you remember to this day the pieces you liked and the ones that attracted some attention.

If rewards come early for the first little successes, then a person will want to practice small steps more. If only big successes attract encouragement and little improvements are ignored, one can become discouraged along the way, *"I'll never be really good."* **It is not the pot at the end of the rainbow that keeps the practice going, it's the next pat on the back or penny in the bank**—and for some tasks, parents need to be frequent and generous with back-pats and pennies.

The most common error when beginning to teach something new is to demand too much for too little. The first steps need big rewards—not necessarily money or tangible goodies, but plenty of encouragement.

"This sounds like bribery," you might say. *"Shouldn't they do most of these things without contrived rewards? Can't they do it just for the love of learning? Some kids are good and do what is expected without 'rewards,' don't they?"*

To answer these questions we need to realize that those good kids *were* rewarded—socially and with parental respect and praise. Some start early and well, with plenty of encouragement. They perform so well that they receive a great deal of praise and a snowballing effect begins that is an advantage for years to come. **If a teen starts off with good encouragement and is well rewarded, he keeps going; if he keeps going, he is further rewarded and so on.**

Snowballing can work the other way also. Some don't receive rewards or attention for the first steps to good performance and learning. They don't expect praise because little was given in the past. If their parents threaten them, they might do just the minimum out of fear, but even the minimum will disappear when the threat is gone.

> **The most common error when beginning to teach something new is to demand too much for too little.**

So without someone providing positive feedback, a teen misses out on encouragement and slows up or stops practicing altogether. Without practice, more opportunities for encouragement will be missed, and even less practice will result. As he falls further and further behind his parents' expectations, any performance that should have been encouraged earlier will be ignored because *"He should have done that long ago."* Now even meager attempts at catching up are discouraged. If his success is viewed as "too late," the "pay" may be nothing. Without some "pay" he will fall further back.

> Stanley: *"These math problems are really hard."*
> Mom: *"You're really getting into some hard stuff now."*
> Stanley: *"Yeah, they take too long."*
> Mom: *"You got the first one, you should show your brother."*
> Stanley: *"Hey, Larry, look at this!"*
> Larry: *"We did those last year."*
> Mom: *"And they were hard, but Stanley got the first one."*
> Stanley: *"I'll try one more."*

Mom's intention here is to show respect for what Stanley has done so far, and a little encouragement to show it off. Larry doesn't help much, but Mom remains on the positive side and Stanley puts in a little more effort.

Does this mean that all successful parents are secret bribers? No. First, these words are unfair because they imply a situation in which a person is trying to corrupt another person so that he or she will do something wrong and usually illegal. Second, we are not involved in "bribery" just because we expect some return for our effort. No one works for nothing. Volunteers don't work for money, but for the satisfaction that is rooted in the reactions of others. The reward may be as subtle as another person saying we are doing well or as obvious as salaries for Congress and fees for doctors and lawyers.

On one occasion a father rejected my suggestion for encouraging his son's homework by saying. *" He should be grown up*

enough to want to do the right thing without some payoff."
When it came out that the father was on strike for more money *and* was getting support from a union strike fund, his defense was that *he was an adult.* With his experience and knowledge he felt he deserved a tangible reward (as well as admiration and respect). **His son, without experience or success, was to take his responsibilities for the love of it.**

So in addition to practice, we need recognition, respect, encouragement and rewards. With all these right ingredients, success will come *and*, along with it, the self-respect.

Taylor told funny stories from his school experiences many evenings at dinner. Family laughter and comments made him feel good, and during supper he trusted his family not to raise embarrassing questions about his school performance. Ellen got a lot of recognition during supper-

> *In addition to practice, we need recognition, respect, encouragement and rewards.*

time too, but it took the form of arguments with Dad. Disagreements were a habit because she received little notice for her accomplishments, and she had learned to start arguments and settle for the unpleasant attention.

Taylor: *"So, John was looking the other way as he went around the corner at the end of the hall, and he ran right into Ms. Letty pushing a lab cart with crickets in a box. Boom! The crickets escaped when the cart bumped over and he said, 'Oh! I'm sorry. I didn't mean to dump your crickets. I hope it doesn't <u>bug</u> you!'"*

Dad: *"What a story! What happened?"*

Taylor: *"John and Ms. Letty were jumping around chasing the crickets and some other students*

> helped too, but some were yelling 'Oh! Get them
> away! Don't touch them!' Everyone started
> laughing."

Ellen: "I don't think it was so funny. Ms. Letty could
> have been hurt and so could those crickets."

Dad: "Don't be a grump. It's just one of those harm-
> less accidents that adds humor to the day."

Ellen: "Big joke!"

Dad: "You ought to lighten up!"

Since we understand that payoffs have a big influence on a
teenagers' behaviors, we can ask, *"How can I support the actions I
want from my teenager?"* and *"How can I get rid of behavior I
don't want by removing support?"*

In Ellen's case, her father could listen and ask neutral questions
as suggested in Step 1, instead of challenging Ellen at the supper
table. Instead of arguing, he needs to *go more than halfway* to
encourage her appropriate contributions. The effort is essential to
change.

When Ellen said, *"I don't think it's so funny. Ms. Letty could
have been hurt . . ."* she signaled the start for her arguing behavior. Perhaps in the previous exercise listing behaviors, Dad could
have decided in advance to control his reaction to Ellen's negative
behavior, then he could have been alerted. His next comment
could have focused on the neutral part of Ellen's remark. Dad
could have said, *"Yes, Ms. Letty could have been hurt and the
crickets squished."*

Ellen: "Yes, and John was lucky everyone was so busy
> catching crickets he didn't get into big trouble.
> Next time maybe he'll look when he goes around
> corners."

> Taylor: *"That's not funny."*
>
> Dad: *"Not funny, but a good idea for John."*

This strategy requires close attention from Dad and that means some planning and singling out of goals as during the exercises at the end of this chapter. The adult thoughtfulness of Dad and Mom can lead to the cure for poor teen behaviors.

Let's look at another example of specific behaviors and incentives that are related to school achievement.

Dan carried home a great report card. He put it between the pages of his social studies book to keep it clean on the way; it had to be neat when he showed it to Mom.

> *"How was school today?"*
>
> *"Pretty good—we got our report cards. Want to see?"*
>
> *"You bet I want to see!"*

Dan brought out the improved card with a smile, and Mom looked over the contents. *"Up in math. Up in English. You didn't go down in anything! Really good! I bet our sessions after supper have helped. You try so hard."*

Mom's support of good behavior was important. She was as encouraging as she could be of Dan's success, and her compliments must have been a motivation for him. Additional credit probably goes to the encouragement in the sessions after supper.

There were two behaviors in this story: bringing home the report card *and* doing homework. The behavior that benefitted from support was the **present** behavior. When Dan came in with his card, he was encouraged, he certainly looked forward to it, and everyone enjoyed it. After supper, a homework session will begin, and Mom will continue her positive attention and focus on the other crucial behavior—doing homework. Dan was getting help in

both places right where he needed it.

Poor report cards and poor homework make up a pair of behaviors. The temptation in this case is to give punishment for poor report cards, with only a hope that the punishment will "spill over" to more homework effort. Another tactic is to try punishment for both report cards and poor homework. This unhappy solution seems to be a trap for bad things getting worse.

The situation requires an upbeat, positive side. We will need specifics about homework added to the lists of the previous exercise—particularly on the positive list. Then we need the exercises at the end of this chapter to find the incentives to make things improve.

Matching Funds and Graduated Allowances

Positive feedback for correct behavior is especially important for teens because they need the message as well as the encouragement. They are not yet sure of the right way to act. Should they try not to be messy or lazy, or is that "uncool?" They lack information as well as motivation.

We all need support and incentives for our actions: pleasant reactions, paychecks, awards, and of course, our own good feelings when we do things we value. Teens are still learning about what good behavior is so they crave a lot of encouragement and payoffs.

A graduated allowance pays off a variable amount depending upon the behavior of the teen. It uses the traditional allowance which is guaranteed and usually unrelated to performance, but guarantees only a small minimum.

Responsibilities are listed for the child and additional amounts can be earned during the week. Each time the child finishes a task, it is recorded on a chart. Each task has a value and the accumulated amount is paid off at the end of the week.

The possible increase in allowance need not be more expensive for the family budget. As money accumulates, it doesn't all have to be spent on amusements. Consider a matching funds program for clothes, for example, where parents provide most of the funds, but for some items they require their child to contribute from his or her earnings.

A Teen's Role in the Family Economy

A system of payoffs can compensate teens for contributing to domestic necessities of the family. An exchange system could be set up where an activity receives some kind of compensation. Psychologists call this kind of exchange a token economy because in many early programs tokens were used to represent the payoff. The traditional allowance is one kind of token economy.

Since an allowance system is an inevitable part of family practice, parents and teens alike should benefit from an allowance based on the effort a teen puts toward self and family care each week. You and your teen could agree about chores which need to be done and how much each chore pays off. That agreement prevents a teen from timing requests for allowance according to the parents' moods.

Now you are ready to discuss chores and payoffs with your teenager. Your teen can record work done on a chart or checklist, using an honor system. This is a chance to show trust.

As the weeks progress, tallies on the weekly allowance chart will become more numerous, and your teen will start saving for shopping. The chart and a payoff time prevent the need for nagging and coercion. When chores are not done by the agreed time, instead of using fines, which undermine confidence in the economy, have the teen make amends, as suggested in Step 8. In this case, "allowance time" should occur with time left in the day for

---

Exercise 3:   Planning the Token Economy

1. **List the chores you think should be done each week by your teen.** Consider your teen's starting level, need to grow, available time, and family work.
2. **List your teen's weekly/monthly/long-range expenses.** Some teens pay for their own school supplies, movies, tapes, and gifts to friends. Others save for big items such as a radio, clothes, a bike, or car.
3. **Place a tentative amount of payoff next to each chore**, considering the minimum wage, amount of time your teen takes to do the work, the teen's expenses, and your own generous nature. This is a chance to be encouraging and fair to the teen and your budget.

---

chores to be done if the teen is disappointed in the week's yield.

Points can be used instead of money. When a teen accumulates enough points, they can be cashed in for a special treat, a small party for friends, a favorite meal, or an outing. However, teens need practice spending and saving money to learn those skills.

We hear complaints that the token economy uses bribery and over-emphasizes money. The concern for explicit rules about money and how your teenagers get their share might seem too detailed and too mechanical. But we all need some compensation for our work, and you are paying your teens for work, not bribing them to get things done. The label, bribe, takes away respect and the positive emphasis on earning rewards by honest effort that we all enjoy.

Always emphasize sincere social rewards as well: *"Well done! Your work helps our family!"* so your teen will value his/her accomplishments in addition to the money gained.

> *Always emphasize sincere social rewards as well.*

Teens will be given their share of family income by some means or other and, as adults, will have to earn their own, so they might as well learn gradually to earn their own way.

Promotions in the Token Economy

Once the token economy is firmly established, other incentives can be added. The most important of these are promotions based on good performance. This allows for duties on the chart to be changed, improved, and modified as the teen grows up. If the teen performs well on some of the more simple and tedious chores, she/he might be promoted to a better set of duties.

Promotions represent higher expectations and emphasize a parent's respect for improved capabilities. If no promotions occur in the token economy, then the system has failed because the teens are not growing up to new responsibilities.

For example, one mother developed a token-economy program to provide an incentive for her son's chores. After the system was applied for several weeks, the son complained that some of the things he was required to do were "kid stuff." Taking out wastebaskets and garbage bags were particularly unpleasant tasks for him. Mom then added a new procedure providing that if he successfully performed the task for 15 straight days without reminders from his mother, he would be promoted to a new task, washing the car. The chart would be changed, and the job of removing wastebaskets given to his younger brother.

The older son eagerly looks forward to this possible change of events because he likes doing anything with the car; the younger son welcomes an additional task, because he wants more opportunities to perform duties for tokens from the system.

BEING "WEIRD"

Why Do Teenagers Do What They Do?

Understanding the reasons behind specific actions can help you influence the direction and nature of your teen's learning.

Why do teens and other people behave the way they do? Unchangeable physical characteristics and early experiences play important roles. People also adjust their behavior to achieve certain payoffs, such as self-satisfaction and enjoyment, attention from others, encouragement, and rewards. Although physical limitations and early experiences are unchangeable, we can change some of the "payoffs" teens receive for their behaviors.

> *The "why" of behavior is easy to see when we describe specific behaviors and their consequences.*

The *"why"* of behavior is easy to see when we describe specific behaviors and their consequences. Instead of leading us to speculate about inherited traits and early traumas, the *"why"* question becomes *"What happens next, after the behavior?"* or *"What are the consequences?"* Kim is irresponsible or Shanna is self-centered. Then what happens? Someone else irons Kim's wrinkled clothes. Shanna's parents help her even though she seldom returns the favor. Those supports may be reasons *for* the poor behaviors.

Where Do the Kids Come up with These Impulses!?!

Parents are often amazed at the variety of behaviors—both good and bad—their children show. If you find it difficult to sort out what good behaviors you want, then you can see how difficult it will be *for them* to find out how they should behave. Of all the possibilities, what will they try first in a new situation? Most of the time they will try what worked best for them last time or in a similar situation. **If nothing comes to mind, they may try out what you do. If it works for you, maybe it will work for them.**

Just as you provide consequences for them, you are also the one they will imitate. Kids may deny it, adults often do, saying we won't do this or that the way our parents did. But then we are surprised to find ourselves acting very much like our parents: *"I can't believe I said that, I sound just like my father!"*

Your parents found the best adjustment for their problems, so you probably went with their choice, and your children will follow you. When your children agree with you, you will support them. That will be a reward, and another habit, good or bad, will have been passed along to another generation of the family tree!

So it's not always genetics, sometimes it's just plain old imitation. As one mother once said to me, *"I can't understand why my children are fussing at each other all the time. I'm always <u>fussing</u> at them about it!"*

> Mom: *"Carolyn really tries hard to be pleasant when any member of the family comes over to visit. She asked Grandma Mildred if she wanted a refill on her coffee and later Carolyn asked her if she was tired!"*
>
> Dad: *"I think she takes her cue from you; you always try*

to make sure everyone is comfortable when company comes. It just rubs off."

In another case, a father and mother came to me for help in dealing with their son whose main difficulty was his disrespect for others, particularly his mother. "Disrespect" was defined as making sarcastic remarks, ignoring direct questions, and insulting people. The father said he thought the mother contributed to the problem by being *"wishy-washy"* and not *"standing up to him, even if she is a woman."* He thought she

> *So it's not always genetics, sometimes it's just plain old imitation.*

probably got this attitude from spending time in *"big conferences"* with some of her *"silly friends."* No doubt Dad's disrespect was obvious to his son and provided a terrible model.

It was easy to see where we needed to start. However, it was a surprise to the father that the place to start was with the example he set for his son. The habit had become strong and the son expected praise and admiration (from his father) for his behavior.

As we will see in Step 10, cooperation and support between parents is needed for extra consistency, but it is also needed as an example to teens in how to treat their parents!

Compulsions and Fidget Behavior

Nail-biting, hair-twirling, nose-picking, and lip-biting are usually maintained partly by parental attention and partly by the absence of something else to do. They are behaviors that fill up time and are occasionally rewarded accidentally by parents.

However, fidget behavior can be more complicated than plain fidgeting. It's fidgeting with a long-term commitment. It happens in the slow, somewhat boring moments of life and almost everyone does it. At first it can be just the random squirming and wiggling of a child. We may say, *"Stop that fidgeting!"* Later on, the little habits develop into hair-twirling, scratching, or ballpoint pen-clicking. Even eating and drinking can develop into fidget (fill-up-the-dull-time) behaviors.

A well-known psychology experiment concerning fidget behavior has been repeated many times. A laboratory white rat is trained to press a lever for food. He soon learns that the food is only given after long intervals—about two minutes. In the mean-time there is little to do but wait. What to do, what to do? A water bottle is available, but the rat has water all the time in his home cage so he is not thirsty. But, faced with nothing to do, he drinks (sound familiar?).

It's not in the rat's nature, or ours, to do absolutely nothing. For humans, doing nothing is embarrassing. So we pretend to read (or something) in waiting rooms, in restaurants, and at bus stops. Many of us wouldn't go to a restaurant alone without something to read.

So the rat drinks. But not just sips. He may drink up to two times his body weight in water while waiting for time to pass! Since no rat has a bladder that big, you can see that the experiment requires regular cleaning chores.

All that was needed to stop our furry waterholic was to shorten the waiting time—down from 2 minutes to 30 seconds. With the shorter interval all the excess water drinking was gone. Pay-offs came more often, there was work to be done, and our rat had no time for fooling around!

So now we have *two* possible explanations for frequent, repeated, annoying behaviors—one, they could be attention-getting and two, they could be fidget behaviors to pass the boring time. The difference is important.

For attention-getting behaviors, we need a strategy that reduces the attention for that behavior, but for fidget behaviors we need to also reduce the boredom of dull moments. Take a little extra time for reflection when you first see the beginnings of a "nervous" habit or a "compulsive" behavior.

Rewarding other behavior that is desirable will be a good strategy in either case, but the reaction to the annoying behavior itself should be a careful one. For attention-getting activities you certainly want to reduce attention, but if it's a fidget behavior, there is all the more reason to see that support and opportunity for more acceptable behavior occur more often.

> *Two possible explanations for frequent, repeated, annoying behaviors are one, they could be attention-getting and two, they could be fidget behaviors to pass the boring time.*

A teen's fidget behavior is due to down time—the lack of anything to do. At least the teen's view is that there is nothing to do. You wouldn't want to get into a *"I'll-bet-you-can't-make-me-happy"* game, but clearly some increase in action is called for.

Fidget behaviors can quickly develop into attention-getting or other reward-getting behaviors. **Now that boredom has brought on the behavior, what reward will it attract?** "Jumping on" fidgeting behavior can be a dangerous parental habit. If the bad behavior thrives on attention, the parent will need a long remedial strategy later. If the behavior is not important let's not make it so. Instead let's look to the situation for a way of enriching the moments. **Any smoker or heavy drinker will recognize the fidgeting aspect of their habit** and tell you that the worst time of temptation is during the low moments—not just the depressing ones, but the boring ones, also.

Your first question about a compulsive behavior then,

should be, *"Is the behavior a problem serious enough to warrant
any strategy at all?"* Your second question should be, *"Is there
anything about the current reactions that could alleviate the
tension and add some enrichment to the situation to "squeeze out"
moments of temptation for fidgeting behav-
ior?"* Along this line, you might consider
what activities you want in the situation and
what opportunities there are for such activities.

> *If the behavior
> is not important
> let's not make
> it so.*

Another strategy frequently used is to
reward the lack of compulsive behavior. For
example, one mother told me she promised a dollar to her son if he
could refrain from nail-biting long enough so that his nails would
need cutting. Because this demand seemed a bit too large for a
first step, her son was also given a quarter for *each one* of his
fingernails that needed trimming because it had been allowed to
grow.

Such a direct contingency upon a compulsive behavior must
be used carefully. There is always a tendency to do more than
state the rule, and nagging ensures that some attention will be
connected to mistakes. As with any attention-getting behavior, in
the child's view he or she is not getting enough attention and has
now found a behavior that seems to alleviate the deprivation. **If
you now come along with a new strategy that sees to it that
your teen's usual solution for getting attention will not work,
then you need to look for a newly designated, desirable behavior to trigger your special attention.**

The new way to appropriate attention should be one the teen
can easily accomplish.

Rhythmic Habits

Rhythmic habits are sometimes symptoms of severe childhood disorders. Autistic children often engage in repetitive behaviors for hours and also exhibit developmental disabilities and impairments in mental function.

Normal children, teens, and adults have rhythmic habits, too. Tapping a pencil, swinging a foot, and rocking to music are common pastimes. These may annoy parents but are probably too trivial to merit a strategy beyond ignoring.

When the habit has become troublesome, most parents can remember it beginning as a less frequent event. **This can be a case of parents trying to fix a non-problem and now they have a problem!** A behavior that started as fidgeting became a gimmick for attention, then a way to express exasperation at the parents. "Getting through to" the parents now gets a reprimand, a kind of attention in a situation where positive attention seems unlikely.

An occasional correction or request to stop the annoying habit is not likely to do much harm if the emotional reaction of the parent can be kept in check.

> Mom: (Rich has been tapping the table with his fork for three minutes) *"Rich, stop that racket—it's a bother when we're eating."*
>
> Rich: "I can't help it."
>
> Mom: (Still in a very quiet tone) *"Well, if you can't help it, how about eating in the other room in a soft chair? Did you finish your science homework?"*
>
> Rich: (Still tapping) *"Yes, it's about DNA."*
>
> Mom: *"DNA. I'd like to see what you did after we're finished. Please don't tap."*
>
> Rich: *"I told you I can't help it."*

Mom is right to provide another direction for Rich's focus. These other topics will have to become a regular part of Mom's habits *before* the annoying habit goes away. She will have to be very steady in her conversation. **If she only comes up with these interests when Rich annoys her, you can see where this will lead.**

Watch Out for Labels That Mean Too Much!

For many years psychologists have searched for solutions to the problems of parenthood. Their searches have usually focused on the reasons children and teens behave—in reacting to parents, siblings, friends, and school. If the reasons were easily known, the solutions could be found. The solutions would make life easier and parenting more enjoyable.

But solutions have been difficult to find because they seem buried in a maze of complicated answers concerning the genes children inherit, the importance of early experiences, and the recent treatment they have encountered from parents and others.

> *Explanations and theories may describe a possible reason for a child's behavior, but you still need practical strategies for action.*

Explanations and theories may vividly describe a possible reason for a child's behavior and may help you understand the situation. That will be helpful in *thinking about* the problem in a calm and loving way. However, you will still need practical strategies for action at the moments when problems come up.

Parents cannot afford the common craziness of doing the same thing over and over but expecting a magical new result! Instead, we could try a *new* reaction based on analyzing the events that produce it and the reactions our teen gets for it. That is, what happens next? **The search for solutions should always return to a concern for the question,** *"What happens next?"*

Concentrating on behaviors and their consequences allows us to discover how to use *our* behaviors to change the behavior of others. The more recognizable the activity is, the more consistent the reactions to it can be. Therefore the child's experience and learning will be more consistent. For example, the broad labels we use for teens, *"She is messy, he is rowdy," "He is hyperactive, she is lazy,"* seem to describe characteristics that are inside the person, beyond our influence. In fact, any mom or dad can influence even these characteristics once they

> *The more recognizable the activity is, the more consistent the reactions to it can be.*

identify them by specific behaviors. Instead of shy, a little thought may focus on, *"Bill doesn't talk much or look at people when he does."* *"Rowdy"* could mean she speaks in a loud voice and pokes people. *"Hyperactive"* might become, *"Reg interrupts his homework by walking around the room every few minutes."* In specific terms, *"lazy"* breaks down to, *"Julie listens to music and naps instead of doing her chores or homework."*

The task of being *specific* about *complaints* is not difficult. Often both parents and teachers have rules about specific mistakes. The challenging part is in listing specifics on the *good* side. Most parents know what to reprimand but fumble with praise on only infrequent occasions. Exercise 4 at the end of this section asks for both lists—unwanted teen behaviors *and desired behaviors*. Lists of these specific teen behaviors will help you plan specific parent reactions—negative when necessary, positive when deserved.

One objective is to influence the specifics and increase the good behavior. A second objective is to send a strong message to your beloved teens that there are many things you *like* about them. The exercise at the end of this chapter will put you on the lookout for sending proper messages. It shouldn't be skipped.

Short-Term Benefits and Long-Term Goals

While sorting out what happens next, both immediate and delayed reactions need to be considered.

Mom: *"Why does she go running out of the house without a jacket? She knows she gets a cold every time!"* (Ah yes, But that's <u>later</u>!)

Dad: *"My friend, George, is just like that at work. He snacks all the time, he's overweight, and he can barely climb a few stairs without panting. Someday he'll be a death-due-to-donuts! Can't he see what he's doing to himself in the long run?"* (That's later, also, and George gives in to the *"right now."*)

Teacher: *"I run two miles every morning. Sometimes it's hard to get started on it, but I feel better afterwards."* (Somehow this teacher resists the effects of inconvenience right now for a better feeling later. How does she do that?)

Brian: *"It's a good TV night, but if I attend every Scout meeting, I'll get a merit patch!"* (Here's a hint about how long-term benefits come to work: there's a *short-term* benefit!)

Behaviors tend to follow the short-term benefits at the expense of long-term goals. But with a few positive experiences, long-term benefits can overpower temporary temptations especially if someone supports the effort. How can a parent help this process of considering the long-term benefits of good behaviors and the long-term problems of bad ones?

The one common parental strategy is to try to talk a teen into considering the long-term. Talk by itself is often not enough as most of us dieters know. We need some symbol of the long-range goal *right now*—a reminder that we are making some progress: a daily chart with marks for successes, a record book, or diary. Teens may need something more concrete such as stickers, buttons, Scout badges or treats. If those little encouragements are given some respect, they can have an effect on the present behavior. Isn't that what compliments from the boss, new titles or privileges at work, promotions, and badges in the military are all about?

> *Talk by itself is often not enough as most of us dieters know.*

Many ideas for some reactions in the here and now are not contrived tokens, badges, or promotions. They are simply people looking for an opportunity to compliment and praise the small steps of good habits. Being so observant and responsive is not easy, but those who do it have good results.

We all know how our morale is elevated by bosses who are positive and supporting and deflated by ones who only react to mistakes. **When work and chores are only for the long-term benefit, a "boss" needs to put in some short-term encouragements that promote the good effort.**

Cures and Changes

The idea of a cure implies that some general change has taken place in the individual. But in the approach here, parents focus on one or two problems, plan some reactions for these and then carry them out. For everything else going on, they have to rely on their reflex reactions and the reactions of others. The general cure will have to come from an accumulation of small changes.

When we visit the doctor, we all hope for a quick and effortless cure, a magic bottle with pills that are easy to take. Changes in child-rearing rarely happen in that quick and easy way. **Bold strokes that suddenly "get through to" a teen are seldom accomplished.** What your teen comes to expect as a result of consistent experiences will make up the long-lasting behavior patterns. **There are no magic bullets.** There's only you and your teen and what your teen does, what you do and, later, what the rest of the world does in return.

The strategies described in this book focus on individual behavior problems. The changes in behavior brought about by these strategies may be relatively permanent, and that permanence can be somewhat ensured by supporting behaviors that you know are likely to be supported by others. For that, you must rely on your ability to observe what results or consequences follow the individual activities that are important to you. Your effort should focus on small problems and emphasize the repetition of consequences.

Practice implies repetition and, in the context of this book, this means the repetition of consequences as well as the behavior.

Making Plans for Non-Behaviors

Be careful when trying to arrange plans and consequences for non-behaviors. Rules that say, *"If you <u>don't</u> do such and such (watch too much TV, act too shy, walk on the flowers, hit your sister) I'll reward you"* are difficult. The time of the promised reaction may be too arbitrary. When does *not* watching too much TV happen?

Better to build your rule around the *alternative* to TV—something that happens at a particular time and gives you an opportunity to support your son or daughter at a particular moment, *"So you're working on your art, it's looking really good!"*

The non-behavior rule not only fails the specific time test, it also fails to tell the teen exactly what to do. *"Karen watches too much TV"* needs to explore what Karen *should* do. Karen's parents would be at a loss to keep her busy every moment but it's a situation where the *extent* of TV is the problem and Karen's parents could plan some encouragement for a few alternatives to the tube.

> *When does not watching too much TV happen?*

Does this mean that Karen's parents should load up on toys, candy, and money to lure Karen away from TV? Probably not. Most parents have found these rewards to have temporary effects—except in the case of money which will become a bigger part of Karen's life soon enough without using it here.

For problems such as Karen's we need to look around for something useful that we might encourage her to do which would have the additional advantage of making Karen feel a little more important. She might be proud of doing some of the drudgery of life. How about dusting, setting the table, cooking, sweeping, cleaning, or painting. Painting? *"But she won't do it right!"* you might say. *"She'll mess it up. Cooking? That must be a joke."*

Of course it's true that you could do any of these tasks better than your teen. To get it done right, do it yourself. But the purpose here is not just the job itself, it's the self-esteem, the learning, and the alternative to TV. **How well the job is done is not a priority.**

Exercise 4: Choose Specific Behaviors

1. **Make a list of the activities *you want your teenager to do.***
    The list can be short for now, but for additional suggestions,
    see Step 6 which describes behaviors that help teens become
    competent adults.

    Be sure that each item on your list is a real action—not an
    attitude or a word of only general description. Instead of
    writing, *"Be more studious,"* list, *"Spend more time reading,
    figuring, writing, and doing math or social studies."*

    It may seem a small difference, but "studious" does not
    happen at a moment so you cannot support it. But reading,
    writing, figuring, and doing other homework happen at particu-
    lar times, so you have opportunities for support.

    Avoid the word, *"not"* in your statements. Instead of *"not
    act bored"* write specifics you think are important such as,
    *"Help with chores, spend time reading, or choose a recre-
    ational activity and stick to it for six months."*

2. **Next, number the actions on your list in their order of
    importance.** The number one behavior is the one you most
    want your teen to do, and the last number is the least important.

3. **Now make a second list of behaviors you dislike and want
    to get rid of.** Again avoid the word, *"not"* in your statements.
    Practice being specific: *"He does not respect me,"* can be
    restated as, *"He says the following bad things to me . . ."*

    When your list is complete, rank order the behaviors
    according to importance. Keep in mind that when you rate
    behaviors very low, they deserve little attention. Possibly
    some bad behaviors are so far down on your list that it isn't
    worth the disruption to react to them at all.

4. **You are ready to compare your first and second lists.** Your first list should suggest new opportunities for you to let your teen know about successes. Select two from near the top of this list for special attention. Be on the lookout for them and use your chances well.

   Your second list will have some behaviors with such low priority that no reaction is justified. Select two from near the bottom of this list and be on the lookout for them. When these unimportant negative behaviors come up, control your reaction, ignore the mistakes, keep the airways clear for better stuff!

Exercise 5:   Find Incentives

1. **Take out the lists you made in Exercise 2 (page 54)**. List several payoffs you can use to support the activities listed in that exercise. Here are some examples:
   * Social comments are powerful and readily available: *"Son, I'm proud of your effort!" "That's my daughter! I'm writing Grandpa about your 'B' on your big science test." "Helping with your brother is a big help to me, too!"*
   * Your teen's allowance can also provide motivation for some items on the list.
   * For some of the items on the list you might use the activity as a time together. Just that extra attention can be a strong incentive to keep up the practice.
   * Privileges can also be used as good incentives: driving the car, for example.

2. **As you expand your ideas for showing support, you might use these reactions against bad performance as well.** For example, you could remove driving privileges when homework

is not done. Giving driving privileges when homework is done
and removing the privilege when your teen falls short may
seem like two sides of the same coin, but there is an important
difference in expectation and emphasis. This might not always
come out in a confrontation when you have to refuse the car
because homework is not done.

However, over the long haul of the semester and the way
the rule is talked about, the message to your teen *will be* different. *Earning a privilege* is something to be
proud of, *avoiding a restriction* is only an
occasion for *relief.*

> *If you only get
> a reaction when
> you do something
> wrong, you can
> keep going, but
> you've got leaving
> on your mind.*

The point of this exercise is to
increase the positive support your teen
hears. Negative rules about what he can't
have if he doesn't do this or that does not
reinforce the message we are trying to build
here. We all need those payoffs. No
employee, spouse, parent, or teen will do their very best without
that positive motivation. All disgruntled employees and unhappy
spouses know that if you only get a reaction when you do something wrong, you can keep going, but you've got leaving on your
mind.

Coaching in
Critical Areas

STEP 5
Give Special Attention to Habits Concerning Alcohol, Drugs, Sex, and Cars

How do you handle the conversation when one of the dangerous subjects come up? No one can tell you exactly what to say, but some intense soul-searching of your own attitudes can help you respond to your teen. The viewpoints presented here can help you build your preparation for these topics and give extra confidence and courage when your rules need to be enforced.

While the most dramatic teen-drug stories in the media involve illegal drugs, statistics tell us that your teen is more likely to abuse alcohol than any of those other dangerous substances. Drugs often produce the most disastrous problems, but in number of abusers alcohol wins. Drug symptoms are listed in the next section, but the first attention goes to alcohol because it's more available and its interaction with other substances can be so lethal.

Alcohol abusers are defined as persons whose drinking habits produce excessive absenteeism from work or school and complaints from friends and family. By this definition one-quarter of our teens are classified as alcohol abusers by the time they reach college. And alcohol-related accidents will still be one of the biggest killers of our teens until they pass college age.

Your teen is picking up messages everyday about alcohol use and abuse.

Don't Send the Wrong Messages About Alcohol and Drugs

1. Don't send the message that alcohol is a problem solver.
Your model is one of the best predictors of later drinking habits. Yet families that approve of moderate alcohol use, for example,

> *Using alcohol for its temporary relaxing effect only postpones learning better social skills.*

Jewish families where wine is a part of religious services, do not show a greater risk of teenage alcohol abuse. The important factor seems to be the message concerning the role of alcohol consumption. *"I've had a tough day; I need a drink!"* is a message that alcohol can solve problems.

2. Don't send the message that alcohol is necessary for social situations. The message that stress or social inhibitions are eased by alcohol is part of the foundation of alcohol dependence. Using alcohol for its temporary relaxing effect only postpones learning better social skills. The habit also becomes entrenched long before the person becomes addicted in other ways. So, for example, many people not yet addicted can't enjoy a party until alcohol has had its effect.

TV and other media glamorize alcohol and imply that alcohol is essential to having a good time. *"Things go better with Bud"* is not necessarily true, as many of us adults have learned.

3. Don't send the message that behavior under the influence of alcohol is somehow more sincere, natural or free. **Teens often think emotional and less thoughtful behavior is somehow more genuine.** The notion that because behavior under the influence is less filtered by inhibitions and thoughtfulness shouldn't lead to the conclusion that the actions are better. Inhibitions have been learned from experience, and thoughtfulness is a human quality.

Intoxication is one of the most common reasons given for unsafe sex in surveys of teenagers.

Parents need to set a healthy model of problem-solving based on the strategies and skills described in previous steps. When teens depend on alcohol to break down social inhibitions, the breakdown of sexual inhibitions will quickly become the next bad habit. Intoxication is one of the most common reasons given for unsafe sex in surveys of teenagers.

Drugs and Self-Esteem

Increase your teen's self-esteem by spending time together and listening to his/her views and concerns. Spending time with your teen sends the message that your teen is a valuable person. A teen who feels valued and capable is less likely to start using alcohol or drugs than teens who feel they have *"nothing to lose."* Recognize your teen as an increasingly capable, valued family member.

Watch the Money. The drug business is about money. Where can an unemployed addict get $75 a day to support the habit? Recruiting new users is one of the best sources for money. Drug pushers look for teen buyers with extra money, so your teen should carry only the needed amount to school or stores. Listen for information about the amount of money your teen has. Encourage putting money away in savings or shift responsibilities such as buying clothes and personal items to your teen. A bank account for a teen may not seem related to the drug problem, but it is, since a teen with extra money is a tempting target for a frantic user.

Observe. *"Tune in"* to your teen's life, habits, and problems. Notice general changes in eating, sleeping, health, and friends.

Check List Number One:
Watch for Changes in Habits

1. Does your teenager need more money than usual, or is money missing from the house?
2. Is your teen spending more time in his/her room with the door closed or locked?
3. Have sleeping or eating habits changed or has irritability increased?
4. Has your teenager changed friends or become secretive about friends?

One mom told me she liked to eat dinner slowly so she and her teenage son could talk. It allowed her to learn about his activities with school and friends. When she saw an

> *Set an example for your teen to follow in the use of tobacco, alcohol, and drugs.*

unexplained change in his appetite, she asked him about it and found out that he had started stopping off with friends at a fast food restaurant after school. She was put at ease about a possible danger sign.

Talk with Other Parents. One dad told me he made a point of frequently calling the parents of the friends of his daughter, Angie. As a single parent he liked to compare his teen's experiences with what others were going through. He liked to keep up on the latest news but was careful not to tell Angie's secrets because he respected her right to privacy. He knew it was an important part of the trust they shared.

Be an Example. Set an example for your teen to follow in the use of tobacco, alcohol, and drugs. Teens copy you much more than you think. Review your habits for the sake of your teen.

Be Informed. As much as you think your teen will never abuse alcohol or take drugs, you need to know the signs of use. Checklist Number Two contains characteristics that all teens have at one time or another. Abrupt changes in these characteristics should, however, increase your curiosity, and if you're not satisfied, you should be suspicious. This is especially true when these changes occur along with the habits listed in Check List Number One.

Check List Number Two:
Watch for Changes in Physical Symptoms

1. Lack of concentration; extreme agitation
2. Red eyes, watery eyes, droopy eyelids
3. Runny nose, increased infections and colds
4. Change in sleeping habits—sleeping all day, up all night
5. Slurred or garbled speech, forgetting thoughts or ideas
6. Change in appetite, either increased or decreased; cravings for certain foods
7. Change in activity level; fatigue or hyperactivity
8. Change in appearance, becoming sloppy
9. Lack of coordination, clumsiness, stumbling, sluggishness
10. Shortness of breath, coughing, peculiar odor to breath and clothes

All teens show some of these characteristics from time to time so these characteristics do not necessarily indicate drug abuse. The difference that deserves attention is *a cluster of abrupt changes*.

> *"John started going with those older kids last*
> *summer and suddenly he didn't care how he looked;*
> *he was sloppy, always sniffing, getting up later and*
> *later, and he lost interest in everything!"*

This mother found drug paraphernalia in her son's room the
first time she looked! The *cluster* of changes in social habits,
attitude, and self-care was enough for her to investigate.

Sexual Adjustment

If sexual *behavior* doesn't seem to qualify for your list of
priority concerns about your very young teen, his or her
preoccupation with the topic should earn it a place on the list. The
body of a pre-teen may still be undergoing sexual development, but
the mind is far ahead.

A parent-coach can help a teen with sexual adjustment by
listening as the teen explores his/her experiences, feelings, and
issues. Total ignorance of sexual matters is not possible today
because of peers and the media. Sex education at school can
provide the objective facts, but your teen's anxieties and
confusions are not likely to be trotted out for all to hear at school.

Of course, sex is an emotional issue, so a parent needs to
examine his/her own feelings before trying to help a teen. Which
topics are you ready to deal with? Dating? Differences between
sex drives of girls and boys? Sex before marriage?
Contraception? Pregnancy? Disease? Building a serious
relationship? Decide what you think is important for your teen to
understand first; then prepare to be a listener your teenager can
count on.

Teens will decide their own sexual adjustments, but parents can influence them. Step outside what you did about sex and seek what is best for your teen. Besides listening, how can you help?

Discuss a dating policy and a policy for going out with a group. The two situations usually overlap these days so you need to set your expectations of your teen in both group and one-on-one situations. What are the acceptable places to go and what places are off-limits? What days of the week are acceptable for dates and what curfews do you have?

It's always a surprise to me how few parents have straight-forward answers to these questions. If they haven't faced up to making a few rules, how is their teen supposed to know what the rules are?

Coach your son or daughter about getting along with another person one-on-one for a whole evening. Explore relationship and sex topics with your teen and keep communication flowing.

One mother told me about a conversation with her daughter that seemed to start with curiosity about how she and her husband decided to have children. But as you will see, the daughter was really looking for information about her own risks. It went like this:

Marie: *"Mom, you and Dad waited a long time to have me and Andy, didn't you?"*

Mom: *"Well, Marie, it was a long time but we weren't waiting."*

Marie: *"You weren't waiting?"*

Mom: *"We wanted children, we just...didn't."*

Marie: *"So it took a long time?"*

Mom: *"Yes, sometimes it does."*

Marie: *"So you don't have a baby right off, right?"*

Mom: *"No, not right off."*

Marie: *"Lauren said you could have a baby after... just*

one time—she's always spouting off."

Mom: *"It could happen right off."*

Marie: *"But it wouldn't, if you were careful."*

Mom had a choice at this point. She could have said, *"Marie, I know what you're thinking and let me tell you you'd better stop thinking about anything like that! You could get pregnant easily, get a disease, and anyway it's wrong to go around thinking about getting into a relationship like that at your age."*

The other choice for Mom is to continue this "objective" conversation, talking about risks and their probabilities. Mom kept the conversation away from a confrontation and Marie eventually asked for her mother's opinion as well as information. That's the best Mom could hope for in this talk. So it went like this:

Mom: *"It's hard to be careful in that situation."*

Marie: *"But if you use the right thing…"*

Mom: *"What's the right thing?"*

Marie: *"Well, you know, a condom."*

Mom: *"Still a chance of getting pregnant."*

Marie: *"Well, how about something else? The pill."*

Mom: *"That works pretty well, but it doesn't protect you from diseases."*

Marie: *"Both then. Why not both?"*

Mom: *"Both is good. Staying on the pill too long is not good."*

Marie: *"You could use timing."*

Mom: *"Not very reliable, that was our problem in having you kids in the first place."*

Marie: *"This is too complicated."*

Mom: *"Well, in a long-term relationship you can work this all out and it's not embarrassing, but in*

> *dating, the practical part is too embarrassing to*
> *talk about and that's where the trouble starts."*

Marie: *"I guess."*

You may still be worried about Marie. The talk doesn't end with much assurance about what she's going to do next. But the talk never had a chance of guaranteeing Marie's future; the best Mom could hope for is to provide more guidance to keep Marie on the right path. This is not a place for an efficiency-oriented set of proclamations. A talk short on facts will only lead Marie to ask someone else.

One mother told me, *"I don't have time for all that dancing around. I just tell them."* I would advise making time for dancing around—take it from something less important. Otherwise, you'll never learn what it was they wanted you to tell them.

Create a Dating Policy with Your Teen

Studies link early one-on-one dating, at ages 13-15, to early sexual experiences. Some parents encour-age going out in groups as an alternative to the one-on-one situation. Talk with parents of other teens for suggestions and support (see Step 10).

If your teen belongs to a club or interest group, their activities provide opportunities for outings with the opposite sex, without one-on-one pairings.

Most teenagers and many adults feel the pressure when going it alone for a whole evening of four or five hours of one-on-one dating. Trying to keep the conversation and activity going well can be an uncomfortable experience.

Teens are usually more comfortable in a group situation where the social demands are neither intimate nor continuous. In a group, you are not always responsible for conversation or ideas of what to do. That kind of social sophistication comes later. But in a group, when things get slow with one person, you can always turn back to the group. On your own and without social competence, it's easy to select a dangerous activity by default.

Coach About Dating Customs

Since Mom and Dad's courting days, customs have changed, but your teenager still needs your guidance to feel comfortable. We've already stressed attention and questions as listening skills between friends.

Your son needs to realize, as old-fashioned as it sounds, that he is still expected to take the lead to plan a successful date. You may be able to help with this when you discuss transportation or car use. A son needs to plan something he enjoys and ask his date about her likes.

A teen can help make dates successful by being honest: *"You choose the show, and I'll choose the snack place for later, but I don't do horror movies!"* or *"I guess we could go to that movie, but I give it a 6. What do you think of the comedy at the other cinema instead?"* Ways to compromise will be learned.

Both persons are probably thinking *"I need to act right!"* and they need to see that the best plan is to let others know about their feelings, likes and dislikes. Then with some high-priority choices handy, an agreement is likely. When your son or daughter leaves for a date, encourage some planning of what they are going to do. Then build confidence with praise for looks and wishes for a good time. Self-confidence is fragile, so no last-minute criticism, no parting shots.

Did you have someone to listen when your outing was good and you wanted to share the experience? Or when it was a disaster and you wondered why things went wrong? Your teen needs a reliable listener. Chances are when he/she comes home to share, it will be a bad time for you to bring up your concerns, so other things will have to wait while "teen-listening-time" goes ahead. Weave in some stories of your own best and worst dates to show that the two of you have common ground.

Set Priorities, Raise Questions and Listen

Parents report success from initial talks with teens when they opened communication lines. The important part, and the hardest part, for the teen, is listening. Parents want to make their cases for postponing sex, but the teen can probably only tolerate one point before feeling frustrated at being the listener.

With Daughters. Mom brought up building ideal relationships with Caitlin while they were walking around the lake. Mom had thought a lot about it and had even written down her ideas. She knew she wouldn't be able to say everything, but she had her ideas in mind: that building a relationship of knowledge and trust with someone of the opposite sex takes a lot of time, time to learn the other person's interests, values, behaviors, goals, and dreams. Trust and commitment increase slowly from small bits of time spent together. The eventual bond of marriage is built on a lot of times of trust and caring.

Mom: *"What do you want from an ideal relationship with a boy?"*

Caitlin: *"I don't know. Gee, I guess respect for me and my ideas. Someone who is there for me, someone who likes sports, and has a sense of humor."*

Mom: *"I think respect is real important too. And trust. I learned to trust your dad when I saw him*

> *every day and we talked, over snacks, between classes."*

Caitlin: *"You and Dad knew each other less than a year before you were married."*

Mom: *'Yes, but we spent time together every day talking about our pasts, presents, and futures. We came to know the real persons under our college student shells."*

Caitlin: *"I'll never find a man like Dad. The guys I know don't begin to have it together."*

Mom: *"Men take a long time to grow up."*

Caitlin: *"They have a long way to go!"*

And Caitlin does too. But she has Mom and Dad to listen and share her journey.

Dad should plan his listening session with Caitlin, too. He wants her to understand that when boys have sex, they don't always feel commitment, whereas girls often think having sex *means* commitment. Also, he wants her to realize that contraception before marriage is likely to be used incorrectly, but teens don't like to hear that, because it implies they're not smart. So instead of trying to get across his whole agenda, Dad will try to do something much harder, be a neutral, encouraging listener most of the time.

Dad: *"In your family life class, did they discuss differences in the sex drive between girls and guys?"*

Caitlin: *"Gosh, we heard more about physical differences than drives. But the teacher did say boys have stronger feelings about sex than girls. Do you think that's right?"*

> Dad: *"Well, different anyway. Boys have sex on their*
> *minds a lot of the time!"*
>
> Caitlin: *"Yeah, the boys make so much of it when someone*
> *says something even a little bit sexy in class."*
>
> Dad: *"Guys can be more inconsiderate and selfish than*
> *girls about sex. It's good to know that."*

If Caitlin continues to find a reliable listener in Dad, he may be able to help her understand her own sexual adjustment and the opposite sex.

With Sons. Parents need to keep the lines open with sons as well as daughters. Boys appreciate dads and moms taking time to listen and ask questions to help their sons' sexual adjustments too.

Before Todd had his first serious date alone, he and Dad spent a weekend camping together. Dad noted the important things he wanted Todd to know:

- If you postpone sex you get to know the total other person without the stress, preoccupation and anxiety of sex with no real relationship.
- Waiting means you can both trust each other about sex, and you don't have to hide what you're doing from friends or parents.
- If you wait for sex, you won't have to deal with an unwanted pregnancy, abortion, or disease.
- The sex drive is a very strong want, but it's a short-run need; building a relationship of trust and caring is both a short and long-run need.

> Dad: *"What does a girl want in going out?"*
> Todd: *"A good time, I guess, and a lot of talking."*
> Dad: *"Just to get to know you."*

Todd: *"I guess."*

Dad: *"You talk a lot on dates?"*

Todd: *"Yeah."*

Dad: *"Do you ask a lot about her?"*

Todd: *"Sometimes. Not much, I guess."*

Dad: *"People like someone who asks them about themselves—just as you like it."*

Dad's on his way to helping Todd learn about relationships by asking questions and letting Todd explore his problem. Todd may even discover that his need is not as simple as just sex, but includes companionship and intimacy at many levels.

Keep Communication Flowing

Questions and stories help keep communication flowing.

Dad: *"How was the date?"*

Todd: *"OK, but Jennifer and I just don't get along so well anymore."*

Dad: *"You're having some rough spots now."*

Todd: *"Yeah, she likes those horror movies. We always seem to do her thing."*

Dad: *"What did she think of your new shirt?"*

Todd: *"OK, I guess. She didn't say. Sounds like she doesn't care, doesn't it?"*

Dad: *"A little."* Dad's listening helped and when Todd is ready, he'll find someone who cares more.

Mom: *"How was the movie last night, Susan?"*

Susan: *"Pretty good. Coming out we started talking to Jim and his friends."*

Mom: *"He's a senior, right?"*

Susan: *"Yeah, and he comes on strong. They gave us a ride back and he was all over me! He's nice though. I wish he'd ask me out, but he won't unless I, you know, do more."*

Mom: *"I had a boyfriend like that once."*

Susan: *"What did you do?"*

Mom: *"Well, not much. I told him where I stood and we got along, but it was always a running battle. He'd try something and I'd always put him off. It didn't last long."*

Susan: *"He stopped asking you out?"*

Mom: *"Yes, we were both tired of the struggle. I dated someone else and 'Come-On-Strong' looked for someone more willing."*

Finding out that Mom went through similar experiences, Susan feels more confident. Let's look at two more cases, Kendra and Derek.

Mom: *"How was your date last night?"*

Kendra: *"Oh, fine, I guess."*

Mom: *"Just 'fine'?"*

Kendra: *"Tom and I always end up in the same old argument."*

Mom: *"Really? About what?"*

Kendra: *"Well, you know, like about how far to go."*

Up to this point Mom has been pretty neutral and not argumentative. But conversations with teens always have a turning point when the parent signals her intention to be authoritarian, or sympathetic and helpful. Let's have Mom come up with a question that keeps the conversation in Kendra's control.

> Mom: *"What kinds of arguments come up?"* (Mom is interested, not angry or opinionated, yet.)
>
> Kendra: *"Oh, he says it won't make any problems."*
>
> Mom: *"No problems? Just like a man! There are plenty of problems. For example . . ."*

Well, Mom has slipped into a lecture mode, and Kendra is probably moving toward the door, so let's take this one back and replace it with . . .

> Mom: *"Well, I guess you think there would be some problems."* (Again the control of the conversation goes to Kendra.)
>
> Kendra: *"Tom thinks there's no problem. Right. For him, maybe!"*
>
> Mom: *"Right."*
>
> Kendra: *"Yeah, it's no risk for him!"*
>
> Mom: *"Being pregnant, you mean."*
>
> Kendra: *"Yes!"*
>
> Mom: *"Good point."*

Now something was said here. Kendra's position is stronger and straighter in her mind. No need for closing arguments. Let Mom and Kendra walk out in agreement. It's the most we could hope for; extracting a promise would not have as great an influence as Kendra's own conviction that she is right.

Talk of sex with an open channel for the teen to talk, discover, and state opinions will result in a less confused person who is more likely to make reasonable decisions.

Mom's talk with Kendra can expand to the general topic of relationships so that the role of sex for good and bad can be understood. How has it worked out for Kendra's other friends?

Let's look at a father-son example.

> Derek: *"Girls can be such a pain!'*
>
> Dad: *"How so?"*
>
> Derek: *"Well, they don't know what they want. They want to go out, but then they get, well, stand-offish."*
>
> Dad: *"They don't want to go far enough?"*
>
> Derek: *"Well, yeah. It's not like we're doing, you know, everything!"*
>
> Dad: *"You don't want to do that?"*
>
> Derek: *"Well, I mean I don't expect it."*
>
> Dad: *"Until later."*
>
> Derek: *"Yeah."*
>
> Dad: *"You know that you could get in a lot of trouble with sex."*

That's too argumentative. Let's give Dad the same chance we gave Mom. Dad seemed to get by the choice between authoritarian and helpful at first, but now he's getting ready to lecture. Dad's last remark starts with *"you"* and it is not hard to figure what's coming. So in Dad's second try let's give him some *"it"* rather than *"you"* statements. That should provide a little less confrontation and a little more learning.

> Dad: *"It can be a lot of trouble."*
>
> Derek: *"Well, you have to be careful."*
>
> Dad: *"You're right. But I was thinking of the social trouble."*
>
> Derek: *"I don't get it."*
>
> Dad: *"Well, don't people think of sex as a kind of permanent commitment?"*

Derek: *"I guess. That was the problem with Tom and Kendra. They broke up in a big argument."*

Dad: *"I guess that's one of the problems. Sometimes sex makes a relationship much deeper for one person than the other. Especially if they barely know each other."*

Derek: *"Well, you should be sure of the relationship."*

Dad: *"It takes time."*

Derek: *"Yeah."*

The "lots of trouble" Dad had in mind in the first reaction can now come up by discussing other people, not Derek. For example, how has it gone with Derek's friends, Tom and Kendra? How does the media handle relationships, sex roles, and "trouble"? Exploring the one-sidedness of TV can appeal to a teen's occasional negative focus. You hardly ever get a close look at a venereal disease infection or a diaper change on TV. Realistic decisions will come from realistic views provided by long, open conversations.

Cars

Mastering use of a car follows the same principles as learning other skills, but your teen places extra value on it. A driving school will help your teen master driving, but you will influence the early practice and a great deal of the long-term habits.

At the first driving session with your teenager he/she can simulate driving. Have him/her sit in the car and pretend starting, braking, and turning the car, to become comfortable with the controls. Talk through a drive around the neighborhood, pretend you accelerate up the hill, pull out around a parked car, and look both ways at the stop sign.

After one or two pretend sessions on the controls and learning permit in hand, have your teen practice driving in an empty parking lot to gain real experience with controls and maneuvering the car. Repeat this step several times before moving to the next step. Plan your route each time before starting the car. Most traumatic moments start with a misunderstanding of what was going to be done:

> Dad: *"Turn here!"*
>
> Teen: *"What? Which way?"*
>
> Dad: *"Right here!"*
>
> Teen: *"Right?"*
>
> Dad: *"No, no, left, right here!"*
>
> Teen: *"Left, right, make up your mind!"*

The next sound you hear in this situation will be unpleasant even if it doesn't include the sound of metal against metal. Review plans before taking off. Also review the rules of the road as they apply to parking lots. The most likely minor accident of teens is one in a parking lot where right-of-way is not obvious, and a lot of backing up is required.

Now, before our new driver gets the idea all of this is for free, set up a matching funds program for gasoline, car servicing, driver's license, and insurance fees. And for self-esteem, use your new driver's help with errands and family transportation.

Driving the Car is a Useful Incentive

A teen's use of the car is an effective incentive for schoolwork or chores. Work out a plan everyone has a stake in and understands. Earned time can be recorded on the refrigerator door and used as the teen needs it. Instead of taking away earned driving time for poor behavior, use alternatives to punishment (see Step 8).

When Jeff didn't do his big English project, Mom and Dad heard about it and postponed his car use that week. When he completed the report and was up-to-date in his work, he was able to use his accumulated driving time.

Oversee Driving Practice

When Tom's family traveled to visit relatives in the next state, he did part of the driving, and when Mom or Dad did local errands, Barb was the chauffeur. Before they had too much time out on their own, these teens gained valuable experience and were encouraged for their good driving habits.

Using appropriate speed is especially important to practice. Excessive speed is the most common cause of fatal car accidents. After Barb drove Dad to the mall and back, he praised her. *"I felt safe with you driving because you kept to the speed limit. Also, when we stopped at an intersection, I noticed you looked both ways before starting again. So many people run the yellow lights now, a green light doesn't always mean the road will be clear for you."*

Mom let Tom know when she felt uneasy about riding with him. *"Leave more room between yourself and the next car. What if he had to stop suddenly? We'd crash into him!"* Over-balance corrections with praise for your teen's desirable habits, to keep a positive feeling about sharing car rides with you.

In spite of your defensive driving model and encouragement of safety, your teen may have poor driving habits. Pinpoint a problem and discuss the behavior you want with your teen. Talk over options to encourage the behavior or limit car use, if that is necessary. Emphasize the desired behavior, but take steps to limit the driving privilege until the teen commits him/herself to the safe driving goal.

STEP 6
Move Toward Treating Them
Like Adults Now

At the beginning, *listening* was the most critical parent skill, now as our near-adult faces dangerous temptations, expressing respect becomes the most critical parent skill.

Beware the "You're-just-not-perfect" Game

"You're the son I hoped I would have!" That's the most important compliment most young men want to hear from their dad, one experienced counselor told me. She said most young men look for confirmation from Dad that they have done right. The fathers looked for it when they were growing up, perhaps are still looking for it, and their sons seek the same.

I think daughters live for the same acceptance, and I'm sure sons and daughters both hope for their mother's approval just as intensely as Dad's.

One father told about how he successfully changed his expectations of his son this way: *"I've always felt I just didn't know where to start with Frank. He always did so many things wrong!"*

"So what did you work on first?" I asked.

"Everything, I guess—all his mistakes. Whenever I had the chance I went after something. But this shot gun approach just made him more and more angry. He thought I hated him!

"When he said he wanted to be treated like an adult, I thought he meant he wanted unreasonable adult freedoms. I guess he did mean that, but when I started treating him like an adult in the sense of leaving out little criticisms, judgments, and petty punishments, our relationship started to change. I sharpened my focus and gave up my expectations for perfect. I took your advice of "Catch him being good," doing right on some little things. When I got realistic about what Frank might do well, he began to improve and we got along better, too!"

Mealtimes can often give a representative picture of how family relationships are going. You might think that if the family counselor came to visit, everyone would only show their best side, but I have found that most people fall back to regular habits before we're done with the soup.

On one family visit, Dad showed me his new super computer. His old one had been passed down to his two sons, and they were busy playing games on it. After the tour of the information highway, we started down to lunch, but the boys wanted to show me their computer also. They had done some clever work with Dad's old drafting program on the old computer. Dad said it was amazing how fast they had picked up the use of the program. The boys immediately switched to showing Dad the latest accomplishments instead of explaining it to me. They zeroed right in on Dad's admiration. Since he was usually generous with it, they always wanted to tell Dad the latest about the computer.

Dad later told me that when his father was fatally ill, he had stayed with his mother who would otherwise have been alone at this terrible time. Near the end his father said, *"You're a wonderful son."*

"It was an awful moment, but it was also a great moment, I only wish he had mentioned it 30 years sooner."

Start at a Level You Can Encourage

The key here is to start at a level where you can guarantee yourself an opportunity to encourage your teen's behavior. Let's say you want your teen to help and to talk pleasantly to a younger brother or sister. Watch for the unusual incident when the teen helps or talks nicely with his sibling. Praise the behavior in a sincere way: *"I noticed how you helped Bobby with his baseball mitt, thanks."*

Recognize the aid even if it was not a big act. It is a beginning and the social support for it will have a powerful effect.

If you do not notice any help or pleasant talk between siblings, you need to suggest a small way in which it can happen. Tell your teenager to help his younger brother (or sister) pump up a tire so the bicycle can be used. Be sure to show honest praise. Until such help or pleasant talk is a habit, you will need to notice or initiate it often and support it with appreciation.

> *Be sure to show honest praise.*

Choose a behavior you want your teen to use. If you decide that spending a longer time working on schoolwork is a desired behavior, give recognition for even the first small improvement in studying. This is a starting level and encouragement should come right away. As the behavior increases you can expand your expectations, as we do with adults in the work place.

What Are Realistic Expectations?

"Mom, can you help me sew this patch on my jeans?"

"Sure, why don't you let me do it? It'll be faster." Oops, this is a missed opportunity for learning by practice. How about replacing this first reaction with a more productive one?

"Sure, you go ahead and I'll let you know when you go wrong." That's better. Now there will be practice—he will not **learn** if he doesn't **do**. But negative emphasis on the possibility of being wrong certainly makes it hard for a teen to feel comfortable. Let's try to improve the chances for a positive outcome.

"Sure, let me baste it into place; then I'm sure you can handle it." Here's a good start; it sets up a situation where the son will practice with a better chance for success, and Mom has a good chance to be encouraging. We need to carefully match a teen's capabilities, needs, and interests to the tasks parents can encourage that will produce the best progress and the happiest experiences.

Psychologists worry about our modern society forcing adult concerns on children too soon. And yes, we shouldn't be tempted to force financial, social, or career concerns on teens too soon as a means of "growing them up." But we can gradually allow teens real practice with increasing responsibilities to help them increase their abilities and self-esteem as they get older.

Tolerate Mistakes as Part of Learning

Parents need to tolerate a teen's mistakes as an essential part of learning new behaviors. Even though errors are a part of learning, they may be hard to tolerate, and parents might be tempted to do the job more efficiently themselves, procrastinating on teaching and disallowing new responsibilities.

Exercise 6: Give Responsibilities and Independence

Take a thoughtful look at the table below and list the responsibilities you can gradually give over to your teen: make the bed,
lunch, and phone calls; arrange rides to activities, make dental
appointments, keep a bank account, choose a summer camp.

Ask yourself, *"How many other responsibilities are important
for my teen to master?"* Make a list and decide which one can
come next.

Exercise 7: Being useful and becoming independent

Fill in the ages you think are appropriate for children and teens
to begin taking these responsibilities. At the start of each new
responsibility there will be mistakes, but through practice,
behaviors will be mastered before the young adult leaves home.

Responsibility	Suggested Age	Your Child (Teen) (What age would you choose?)
Clean-up room	4	
Make bed	6	
Select clothes to wear	7	
Bathe frequently	8	
Cook meals (with help)	9	
Use allowance without coaching	9	
Do homework (no nagging)	10	
Choose bedtime	11	
Eat at meals	11	
Save and spend money	11	
Plan and cook meals	12	
Buy clothes	12	
Do own laundry	12	
Decide hobbies and sports	13	
Choose summer camp	13	
Decide evening schedule		
Play, bedtime, etc.	10	
TV, homework, etc.	14	
Decide hours on weekends with limits	15	
Choose weekend hours	17	

Mom tolerated a half-hour of mistakes and spills to finally hear Keith say: *"OK, Mom, I'm putting my cake in the oven!"*

Mom: *"Great. What temperature?"*
Keith: *"350 degrees, I'm setting it now."*
Mom: *"Keith, why don't you wait just a minute or two for the oven to warm. Then the outside won't be crusty from having the heat on so long at the beginning."*
Keith: *"Oh. That's what 'preheat' means in the recipe?"*
Mom: *"Right. What a treat this will be with supper!"*

A parent can learn to tolerate the inconvenience of allowing a teen to make mistakes and improve with practice when trying is viewed as a sign of growing to adulthood. Give responsibility now, gradually, not abruptly on the steps of a college dormitory or in the back of a church just before a ceremony. And with each step keep the praise and incentives handy.

"When are You Going to Start Treating Me Like an Adult?"

Kids changing into adults can be so demanding! They are horses at the starting gate, anxious, often aggravated, pushing at the restraints that keep them back. When can we give in to their demands and which restraints should go first?

Fortunately, the analogy to the horse at the starting gate ends when you consider how many different starting gates we have for teens and that we can close and re-open many of them. We don't have just one moment to start the challenge of adulthood, but we do need to start opening some doors for the sake of practice and of giving our teen a feeling of importance and accomplishment.

As teens grow they are expected to take added responsibility for their own care and to learn skills needed to survive as happy, independent adults. They are also expected to contribute to the family. For a person still clinging to much of childhood, these expectations add up to a lot of worry and confusion.

If the responsibilities are begun early so they can be added slowly, your teen struggling to be an adult can be proud of new capabilities instead of anxious about new demands. Capabilities lead to usefulness which leads to contentment with one's self as a person who carries some of his own load.

> *Capabilities lead to usefulness which leads to contentment with one's self as a person who carries some of his own load.*

At any age after the toddler years, a person's feeling of self-worth can be improved by practicing self-reliance and helping others. Skills learned now will be a source of pride and will be useful now and in adult life. The self-esteem gained from new competence and appreciation from others is important to happiness.

Mastering survival skills also brings rewards in the short and long terms: school skills benefit life-long learning; skill and understanding in dealing with friends now benefit later relationships, and responsibilities now benefit later career plans, success at part-time jobs, and time and money management.

As their skills develop, teens' concerns become more similar to ours every day.

Parents Become Coaches

Teens still need a lot of help from their parents, but they need a different delivery system than when they were children. Parents need to adjust their parenting styles to their teenagers' growing sensitivities about taking increasing control over their lives and discovering their own solutions to life's demands and problems. Parents represent a decreasing portion of their teen's experience but have more advice to give. The parent's role is changing from leader and provider of consequences to companion and coach.

An effective coach provides practice and also advice from the sidelines while the consequences come from the other players. A coach is a good observer, listener, planner, enabler, storyteller, and model. Observing and listening can reveal a teen's needs, and the parent-coach can provide more help to his or her teen's understanding of what's going on. Without careful listening, coaching teens is difficult. It's like running a practice without knowing what happened in last week's game.

Good coaching also uses storytelling and companionship as pleasant ways to pass along experiences. Stories are less threatening than straightforward advice. They set out alternatives and work well with other activities.

> *A coach is a good observer, listener, planner, enabler, storyteller, and model.*

Practice can have its ups and downs. At times teens will be optimistic, ready to enjoy moments of life and set aside responsibilities (Bumper Sticker: *Let's Party!*). Paradoxically, at other times they are pessimistic, less confident in their abilities, and negative about nearly everything (Bumper Sticker (same car): *There is No Gravity, the Earth Sucks!*).

The same cycles are common in adults. Parents who recognize the temporary nature of both extremes can remain calm, providing a steady influence for realistic attitudes and opportunities for lessons to learn. The main role of a parent-coach here is to hold a reasonable view of life while the younger members of the family swing from side to side.

Self-Esteem is Learned from Your Parents

How well does your teenager like him or herself? A person's value of self is always a concern, but in teens it's nearly a preoccupation. High self-esteem builds confidence, productivity, and a resistance to risky temptations. A teen who can say, *"I'm a valuable person,"* will resist self-abuses such as alcohol, drug abuse, depression, and self-degrading sex.

So another role for parents is to enable the teen to learn by doing, to provide practice so that the teen's value of him or herself is increased. For example, Elsa's dad noticed that Elsa spent a lot of time tapping on the table and listening to rock music. She moved around the house a lot, but didn't focus on any satisfying activity. When she mentioned the school band and drums, Dad encouraged her to look into it, talk to the teacher, and learn about what was required. Elsa and Dad went out to buy the instrument together. The project involved some parental

> *High self-esteem builds confidence, productivity, and a resistance to risky temptations.*

coaching, some doing on the part of Elsa, and some direct parental help from Dad.

When Brian's school backpack was beyond repair, Mom didn't run out and buy one. She said he should check around on his own to compare values and prices for a new pack. Then they went together to make a selection—some coaching and help with transportation but also practice for Brian.

As teens experience success or failure at coping with the world's demands and their own ambitions, their self-esteem follows the roller coaster. Having less experience with the ups and downs than we do, they can reach extreme opinions about themselves, inflated or depressed. Their mood changes can be deeper than those of thicker-skinned adults.

Parents can help teens learn to improve and maintain high self-esteem. Our most helpful influence is the model we set of feeling good about ourselves. Share your highs concerning your own accomplishments and in some small way compliment your teen every day for his/her strengths and achievements. Encourage your teen to praise his/her *own* accomplishments and concentrate on the strengths of others.

Often your example of just being active will be imitated and helpful. *"Whenever I feel down, I shoot some baskets."* Activity is therapeutic—if we can get it started. Teens gain satisfaction from an activity that interests them: a hobby, school assignment, or spending time with others who have common interests. Special experiences such as a part-time job can also increase satisfaction.

Using these guidelines can help your teenager gain and maintain high self-esteem.

Mastering Self-Care

Confidence and independence increase when teens assume responsibility for their food, hygiene, grooming, room care, and language. Teens may not like making their own school lunches at first, but they will feel more capable and grown up when they do it.

Eating. If parents have not already allowed food choices from balanced offerings at mealtimes, without comment and coercion, the teenage years are not too late to start. In the short term teens may make poor selections, but presented with healthy choices and using the parent-coaches as models, they will usually select an adequate diet.

Grooming. Peer pressure usually makes a teen adopt accept-able grooming habits. Choosing unusual hairstyles and clothing may be calls for attention and help, or they may indicate concern for fashion. Within reason, it is probably best not to create a confrontation over fashion and style. Consider how you would react to an adult visitor, with respect to the individual's grooming choices. When teens assert themselves through unusual clothes and hairdos, parents need to see it as growth toward adulthood and not a reflection of their own values.

A teen needs to make clothing purchases. This is an opportunity to make and follow a budget. Along with clothes selection comes care. Show your teen how to use the washer and dryer. Make a check list together to specify what clothes are washed how and when. The checklist can also reduce the nagging.

Room Care. Sometimes teens love to fix up their rooms to their own tastes and the variety (some would have a less complimentary name for it) is remarkable! Encourage your teen to select his/her own furnishings, as much as possible, with your help on shopping.

If a young person has gradually learned to pick up clothes, make the bed, dust, and vacuum, it's time for him/her to take over the total job of room care. Social rewards can be very effective, but concrete rewards may be necessary to get the job done.

Before a positive incentive is worked out, parents will have to make an important judgment. How important is a minimum clean-up and how often do you want it done? An answer to these "value" questions will lead to an easier decision about how to do the encouragement part and avoid unpredictable blowups when Mom or Dad visit the room. If the request is to be small and infrequent, then just a little support and encouragement might be enough. A major cleaning every week may require something more concrete.

A clean-up check list spells out the little things, chips away

resistance to an all-or-nothing effort, and pays off at an agreed
time. What is clean enough for the payoff? The one who has to
live with the room the way it is should have the most say. Some
allowance should be paid for all parts completed.

Language use is modeled, but extremes picked up from peers
or the media can become a habit. Coach Dad told a story from
work about losing respect for his boss when she used foul words,
and Coach Mom told of her soccer teammate who was high on her
scale until she used a lot of profanity arguing at a game. Family
members were fond of repeating the remark of a favorite short
teacher who stood up to a tall student when he used bad language.
She said, *"Profanity is a sign of a limited mind."*

Learning Adult Survival Skills

Beyond self-care, teens are expected to master life skills
essential to their happiness and independence during their teen and
adult years: schoolwork, social relationships, recreational
activities, career plans, part-time jobs, and money management.
Help with schoolwork and social relationships has been discussed
in Step 3, but other skills such as time management will be a part
of a teen's adjustment.

Recreational Activities. Parents often complain to their teens,
*"If you can't go out and spend or eat, you think there's nothing to
do!"*
With many adult physical capabilities and a great deal of
information about all the opportunities out there. Equipped teens
are ready for action and adventure. Chores can fill in some boring
moments in a teen's life, but where are the little successes that
come from hobbies and recreations?

Teens need help developing satisfaction from their activities. A mom who enjoys tinkering with her car is a model for her teenager as surely as the father who loves knitting sweaters. Encourage a teen to choose two school or community activities, clubs, or pastimes that follow his/her interests. This is a time for the teenager to take control and make choices. You can share the cost for fees and supplies and provide transportation to events. Generosity will pay double dividends when helping a teen learn new interests. Recognize effort and achievement as your teen pursues his/her interests.

> *Generosity*
> *will pay*
> *double dividends*
> *when helping*
> *a teen learn*
> *new interests.*

TV is popular with many teens who look forward to their favorite shows as recreation or an escape from problems or boredom. While relaxing for a half-hour of TV, teens can learn much that is worthwhile.

But teens have a tremendous need to develop skills by doing, by interacting with people or things, not through the passive activity of staring. So work with your teen to agree on limits for TV viewing; be available as a companion to listen and do alternative activities together that you both enjoy, and help your teenager find active interests to replace TV.

One family controlled TV time by keeping it off on school afternoons and evenings, unless a parent OK'd turning it on. Teens in that family pursued swim team, soccer, piano, ballet, and raised a seeing-eye dog. The swim team experience led to summertime pool jobs. A lot of parent encouragement and transportation helped these teens start and continue their skill-building hobbies.

A Part-time Job

Just as hobbies can be therapeutic to a teen, an outside job can fill spare time in a worthwhile way. A job can help a teenager apply learning from home and school, such as ways to get along with a boss and co-workers, organize time and materials, communicate with the public, and be dependable.

Seven out of ten jobs filled every day come from grapevine leads, so a teen needs to let people know he/she is seeking a position. Encourage a teen to be selective. Since a teen learns what he/she does, the tasks of a part-time job should be worthwhile. Some positions require too many hours at the wrong times so schoolwork suffers. Others are too isolated and repetitive.

An outside job can mean less help with home chores, so plan to lift some of those requirements when your teen starts his or her first job. There is bound to be increased independence, so discuss hours and chores expected, and be extra encouraging for behaviors you agree on. Consider, *"What would be fair if I had an adult boarder?"*

Of course an adult boarder would take care of his/her own chores, but would also have special hours, friends, and a job. The teen is reaching for adult responsibility and independence, but unlike an adult boarder, your teen still needs your support, coaching, and limits.

Managing Money

As a teen's allowance or job earnings grow, provide new ways for it to be spent besides for the teen's own amusement and stomach. Teens can contribute to expenses for birthday gifts and the family car and start a savings account for a long-range purchase. A matching funds program for buying clothes lets

Exercise 8: Career interests and strengths.

Psychologists tell us that teens who have a career goal are more likely to go on to complete their education and stay clear of drugs, crime, and teen pregnancy than those who have no long-range plan. The goal extends the teen's present interests and abilities even though it may change along the way.

1. **Have the teen list his/her ten strongest interests**.
    Examples: nature, health, music, soccer, computers, work with wood, cooking, helping people, business, and politics.

2. **Now have the teen list his/her ten strongest abilities.**
    Examples: organization, grooming, art, math, reading, understanding others, working quickly, persuading others, working alone, and mechanics.

3. **Have the teen list five places in the nearby area that have jobs related to each area of interest and strength.**
    An example for music would be: library—audio visual librarian; record store—clerk; piano store—salesperson; music pavilion—booking agent; school—music teacher.

4. **If your teen is interested in a particular career, you might find a friend in that career who will talk about it to your teen.** I know one mother who, when her daughter said she wanted to own her own business some day, invited friends who had their own businesses to a dinner party and a discussion about owning their own business.

These exercises increase teen understanding of themselves and parent understanding of when to praise. Help a teen make a resume and consider part-time jobs related to his/her areas of interests and strengths.

parents and teens share costs, giving a sense of responsibility in selecting clothes and caring for them.

Extra money should create opportunities for teens to expand control and responsibilities for their own lives. They can begin to cover their day-to-day expenses, not just acquire money they spend for special things. It is cruel training to allow a teen to reap family benefits in the household while paying nothing in return.

A teen with too much money is a dangerous problem! The teen may have worked for, and have a right to spend the money, but some things should no longer be free for the newly rich. A teen can begin to pay for transportation, extra clothes, and entertainment. For the young teen, however, food and room are part of family sharing and security. They should not be paid for by a teen until he/she completes school and has a full-time, self-supporting job.

Teen Contributions to the Family

Parents should gradually expand the teen's responsibility in helping with family decisions, entertainments, and chores. A continuing emphasis on membership in the family confirms the teen's roots and value as a family member.

Sharing decision-making with a teen provides practice with a skill that will be useful for a lifetime. Teens have already gained experience in creating family norms, rules, and consequences. It is rewarding to them to share in planning family purchases, trips, and chores.

How can family members spend time together and yet let everyone do something he/she enjoys? A family meeting in advance of the event can help. It can build excitement about family outings and allow each person to have a say in some aspect of the plans. For example, a trip to a different city might include a side trip selected by each member: visits to a museum, a landmark, a cemetery, a famous store, and a show. A lot of conversation about the choices will add to the anticipation, so instead of a passive, backseat passenger, we might have an excited learner. Afterwards, everyone will still be talking about each other's choices.

Now, after we get back, how can we split up the family work so everyone shares? Input from everyone makes the plan for sharing work a winner. Try assignments, then evaluate and make changes. Enthusiastic cheering and payoffs keep family members motivated. Responsibilities for teens might include shopping, putting away groceries, preparing meals and cleaning up, cleaning house, and caring for the yard and car.

It's an exciting, challenging time when teens reach for adult privileges and responsibilities. Parents improve their teen's chances for happiness and success as adults by gradually allowing them to master self-care and survival skills through contributions to the family.

Making Rules Together

Making rules together means getting household members together to talk over their needs, feelings, and actions and then to turn them into livable agreements.

When poor teen behavior occurs, such as not doing homework, try out one of the alternatives to punishment discussed in Step 8. But if the wanted behavior doesn't come and you give it high priority, then it's time to discuss the situation at a family meeting and make a rule together.

Teenagers and younger children are very capable of under-standing and discussing situations important to their lives and families. Everyone in the household old enough to participate should be at the family meeting.

Mom and Dad were upset about a call from Greg's math teacher. She said Greg had not done homework for a week, so the parents focused on planning for a change in the long term. Dad brought up the problem at lunch.

Dad: *"Greg, your math teacher called to say you need to do your homework. You're getting a deficiency because you haven't done homework for a week."*

Greg: *"That math homework isn't important. I already know how to figure it. My other assignments are the ones I need to do. I can't spend any more time on busy work!"*

Dad: *"Greg, we will have to discuss this more, but tonight I want to see your assignment when it's done, before you spend time on other things."*

Preparing for The Family Meeting

While Greg did his assignment, Mom and Dad discussed the math homework situation. Before a family meeting, an adults' preliminary session is important to air views and feelings and to explore possible solutions to suggest in the event that the teen doesn't come up with realistic proposals.

During the pre-meeting, adults need to emphasize specific actions and realistic levels of behavior and practice communication skills they want everyone to use during the meeting.

Greg's reaction to the call gave his parents ideas about ways to support his math work. He needed to be persuaded about the value of math homework and rewarded for doing it.

Both Mom and Dad would share with Greg their belief in the

teacher's assignment; she was the expert. They decided that one-half hour of math problems a night was a crucial part of learning to work hard and accurately and applying skills to problem-solving. They would tell Greg that part of earning a living is doing work you don't want to do. Practice at self-discipline enables you to do it. You can imagine what Greg's cynical reaction to such philosophy will be, but it may still ring true and have an influence.

They also examined what they were already doing to encourage Greg's homework behavior, and what needed to be done? They focused on providing more concrete rewards for doing math homework. They discussed different options and decided to give points. for every assignment completed. Greg could then use those points toward a movie or other treat. They also decided to share math and logic puzzles and to ask math-related questions, *"Greg, what did you learn?"* and *"Give us a problem to solve."*

They would tell of ways *they* applied what they learned to their life situations, to show the value of his skills. For instance, Mom would tell her story of not wanting to do math homework as a teen, but finally overcoming the math problems one by one. From practice she found quicker ways to do the work and it became easier. Because she finally succeeded in math, she went on to courses using higher calculations, and eventually, a science career.

After Greg showed them an improved report card, they would celebrate his effort with a special meal.

When they discuss all this with Greg later at the family meeting, he might have better suggestions, but at least Mom and Dad now have a positive plan to offer.

The Family Meeting

Young people at a meeting will respect the outcome to the extent they see it taking their needs into account. It takes time to listen to every person so allow an ample period. When family members start repeating what others have said instead of providing new input, you have probably covered the situation.

A regular weekly meeting can be helpful for airing concerns before they reach the problem stage. The rules and consequences the group agrees on may need reworking later, but be encouraged that practice will improve everyone's skills and productivity.

Step 1 concerning communication skills needs plenty of application at these meetings. Also, parents should not push for or expect solutions at every meeting.

When Greg has an opportunity to set policy and abide by it, like most teens and younger children, he is likely to take responsibility seriously. Parents need to make clear the importance of the situation in the short and long runs and follow up with a discussion of adjustments at future meetings.

Reasons need to be clearly stated. For example, if parents don't want Greg's older brother John to go out with friends more than one night a weekend for several reasons, they need to say so:

> *"We don't want to have to worry about your safety more than one night a weekend."*
> *"We think studying one weekend night is important."*
> *"And we want you to spend time with the family doing something special some weekends."*

All family members need to communicate their views of an event or problem, exploring alternative solutions to a situation and suggesting rules and consequences that are reasonable. If parents

listen well, the keys to a workable solution can be discovered.
Teens have a strong sense of fairness, but if teens
do not participate appropriately, parents may
need to postpone the agreement or set a
temporary solution, to be adapted as needed. An
ideal discussion raises issues, explores ways to
handle them, and then postpones decisions until
everyone has had time to mull over the whole
matter. During the interval between sessions,
reservations and shortcomings may surface.
When a final agreement comes, it will be more
realistic because of the added consideration of solutions.

> *If parents listen well, the keys to a workable solution can be discovered.*

Fat Cats

Cats seem to be one of the best animals at taking human care
for granted. **Give them food, housing and a warm pillow and
they can ignore you for days.** Teens sometimes take a similar
attitude. During a moment of rebellion, a teen can act on the false
idea that she is perfectly capable of making it on her own. Like the
cat, she has been misled by a family situation that provides most of
the essentials of life free and with no fanfare. You too could make
it on very little if room, board, clothing, medical, and educational
needs were free! The fat cat problem develops from too few
demands for the teen to care for herself and too few requests to
contribute to the family as much as she is capable. **It's time for
more realistic responsibility. But when you give more
responsibility you will need to add more incentive also.**

Incentives for Added Responsibility

In a more perfect world, everyone would do the right things for the right reasons. We wouldn't need special incentives such as paychecks, bonuses, benefits, or parents using the right reaction. The work would be done because we all know it needs to be done.

But in the real world, all dieters, regular working folks, and exercisers know that free-floating motivation is hard to maintain. We either keep going in order to avoid the negative reinforcement, or some positive reinforcement better be in the offing.

Concrete rewards may also be needed when laziness becomes habitual and resistance to change so strong that we need contrived rewards to make even small steps in progress. For example, to improve the homework study habit, you might adjust the weekly allowance according to the amount of homework done. Some allowance is coming the teen's way anyway, and there is important school work to be done, so the real world might as well start right here—the work and the pay go together.

Set the limits, both minimums and maximums, so that you can't be cornered into an unreasonable position such as allowing *no* money if no homework gets done or having to pay too much if all the homework is done. You will want to keep it simple, but without stated limits you'll be tempted to give out undeserved money or have to refuse to pay up for a sudden burst of activity.

It will be better to set limits at the beginning—say a $3.00 minimum and a $10 maximum. The practice is the most important thing going on in the teen's life, so let's give practice some importance. We guarantee the minimum by saying, *"The $3.00 is for every week, but I'll add a dollar for each night your homework is all done, and two extra for a whole week of successful homework nights."* You could tie the definition of "homework done" to pages of workbooks or the teacher assignments or time spent on homework each night.

With this amount of structure, you'll avoid being an ogre who won't give any allowance, and you'll avoid extravagant payoffs for bursts of activity. After a few weeks, you may want to add special incentives for some subjects or change the definition of homework done," or add an extra pay increase for special efforts. All rules are subject to change.

One of the keys to success in using incentives is to make very reasonable requests, especially at first. These requests should not be based on what *should* be done but on what *has been the usual.* An incentive for doing a half-hour or hour of homework for a teen who has not been able to stick with it for 10 minutes in the last three months is doomed to failure. Start at the current level of the teen now, establish his/her confidence, then the requests can be increased.

> *The real world might as well start here— the work and the pay go together.*

On day one, you want to guarantee that you will get an opportunity to use your incentive! Plan an incentive for a performance not only within your teen's ability but within his/her inclination as well. For example, you might ask that only one page of a workbook assignment be completed before a whole half-hour of TV is approved. The pay-off is so attractive, and the price tag so small that a success is likely.

With small successes "in the bank," we can start a progression toward the amount of homework required before the reward is available. The increments should be small enough to allow a smooth and easy increase in effort.

You must be careful when selecting "less logical or materialistic" rewards because they are usually not a natural benefit of the behavior, and the time will come when your children will be on their own to be motivated by other less generous people. This means that your encouragement, admiration, and praise need to remain a major part of the rules even when concrete rewards are used. Your reactions send the message of the importance and usefulness of the activities you support. You hope that your target objectives are likely to be supported outside the family in a way that is at least enough to keep your child on the right path.

The activities that other people support and believe important are probably the same as yours. Chores such as washing the car, mowing the lawn, painting, cooking, and shopping are some of the easy ones. A young person usually values the same activities even though it may not be "in" to say so.

The teen's habitual attitude toward chores should not mislead parents. Even children who moan and complain when asked to pitch in, still grow a little when they *do* pitch in. Everyone wants to feel competent and able. **So when you ask your teen to do chores, take heart in the fact that the advantage goes far beyond getting the chores done. As a matter of fact, the boost in the teen's self-respect may be the most important outcome!**

Now as you allow your offspring to take part in adult activities, remember to include the fun parts of the job and not just the less desirable ones. When washing the car, she should get to use the hose as well as scrub the wheels. When shopping for food, he should be allowed to pick out a goody as well as get the soap.

One last caution concerning the first efforts to support good behavior: the proof of a little success is in the daily and weekly changes, *not* the immediate reactions of the kids. Remember kids can be very pessimistic about your power. This pessimism may stem partly from their own feeling of powerlessness and partly from a desire to discourage you from trying to influence them. Don't buy it. The proof of change is in the longer term reactions and adjustment.

A second related tactic of your kids may be to belittle the *consequence* as too weak to do any good. The power of consequences is in their accumulated numbers. Small compliments and encouragement, *"You're running the laundry through by yourself? You really are growing up!"* or *"Gerry, why don't you call in the pizza order, you're getting so good on the phone."*

Every penny in the bank adds up—don't be talked out of it, just say (or think), *"Let's see how it goes."*

Planning Reactions
to
"Almost-Grown-Ups"

STEP 7
Avoid Frequent Punishment and
Its Disadvantages
(What are the Results of a "Get Tough" Policy?)

Punishment is a tempting strategy when bad behavior demands immediate reaction, and the long-term relationship with the teen is temporarily unimportant. But punishment doesn't deliver the needed information about what a teen needs *to do*. It is not as effective or pleasant as other alternatives.

For a teen to grow into a happy, independent, productive adult, the family needs to be a place where training through trial-and-error is encouraged and guided. This is the opposite of what is created when punishment is used.

Advice from "Get Tough" Uncle Harry
is Off the Track

"You're too easy on the kids! Let me have them for a week. They'll shape up after a couple of swats from their Uncle Harry!" Nancy and Martin are a sister and brother team that started their act

when they were five. Now in their teens they know all the buttons
to push to get the reactions they want. They're still playing their
game of *"Let's-see-how-much-we-can-get-away-with."* They
either conspire to work their parents up or they bug each other and
get parent attention as a bonus. Any suggestion to Nancy or
Martin by their parents that they do *"something useful"* is rejected,
perhaps because that would mean the game would be over.

Most of the relatives, including Uncle Harry, think they could
fix the Nancy-and-Martin problem with stern talk and extra
punishments—restrictions or removed privileges. Uncle Harry
thinks he would somehow use punishment more effectively and
more consistently. **He's on the wrong track for several reasons.**

Reason #1:
Uncle Harry's Hard-Line Approach
Will Be, Must Be, Inconsistent

The first problem with Uncle Harry's use of the straight punishment rule is that even Uncle Harry cannot, *and should not*, be
consistent with it. Punishment would be too inhuman without the
inconsistencies of warnings and threats.

> *Punishment is too inhuman without the inconsistencies of warnings and threats.*

If Uncle Harry's reactions could be as
consistent and quick as, say, an electric shock,
he might make some short-term progress.
Wall outlets and lamp sockets will
consistently punish you without warning; they
don't hesitate because you look cute trying to
be "devilish." They don't think you've had a
bad day or haven't been reminded lately of
what will happen if you touch them. We get
none of this consideration, and we all stay away from them.

But Uncle Harry is not a wall socket. Out of love and

sympathy, neither Mom, Dad, nor Uncle Harry can resist preceding punishments with the warnings and threats that become part of the game. When the kids were younger, spankings were used. But you can't spank the big ones and anyway, even spanking would have to include lots of warnings.

> *Not surprisingly, most "mean" teachers think the students in their classes are not very smart.*

Parental consistency is always desirable and basic to learning. The lack of consistent reactions, on the reward side, leads to confusion and slows the pace of progress. The inevitable inconsistency on the punishment side brings on additional problems. Remember that "mean" teacher you had in school? He, or maybe it was a "she," used punishments, reprimands, sarcastic remarks, put-downs, and embarrassments whenever the kids deviated from the desirable, and sometimes even when it seemed the kids had done nothing wrong! I bet you hated that class!

A student's greatest fear is to be embarrassed in front of the class. With "Mr. Meany," you just couldn't be sure when you might trigger an embarrassing reaction. *All* behaviors (even volunteering right answers, suggestions, or questions) were reduced because you and your friends just wouldn't risk it. Not surprisingly, most "mean" teachers think the students in their classes are not very smart.

When punishment is uncertain, students become very cautious, especially when they are around the teacher who punishes. Around other people, bad behavior may increase to let off the oppressed steam or just to somehow even the score.

Parents also can fall into the "mean teacher" trap, and their children may learn to behave whenever Mom threatens or looks mad. As Mom realizes this works she may take up "looking (and acting) mad" most of the time. Parents in this pitfall soon find that "looking mad" won't do, and they have to act "really mad." **Now Mom has been pushed up a notch toward becoming a behavior problem herself!**

So for Nancy and Martin to grow into happy, independent, productive adults, they need alternative activities that make the *"Let's-see-what-we-can-get-away-with"* game unimportant. Mom and Dad need to catch opportunities to encourage the kids. They also need to sharply limit punishment and use alternatives such as allowing the kids to make amends for mistakes as we do adults. More on alternatives in Step 8.

Carrying out all of this is much more difficult and requires much more planning than hard-headed Uncle Harry's idea of *"thrashing it out of them."*

Reason #2:
The Punishment Trigger is Often Parent Feelings, Not the Teen's Behavior

In most parenting situations, punishment is a dangerous practice because it is likely to be more related to the frustrations and moods of the parent than to a teen's mistakes. Frequent use of punishment, when Dad or Mom have had it "up to here," usually results in a teen more interested in the moment-to-moment mood of his parents than he is in his own rights and wrongs. So Martin and his sister become manipulators who know that as long as they don't push too far, they're safe. Most punishment is given because the *parents* have reached their limit of frustration and accumulated disappointments. Martin and Nancy can better predict punishment

> *Punishment is a dangerous practice because it is likely to be more related to the frustrations and moods of the parent than to a teen's mistakes.*

by watching their parents' emotions than by respecting agreements. Now the parent-teen relationship will suffer because the punishment practice tempts the teen to react to the parent with disrespect, silence, deceit, and avoid him or her altogether whenever possible.

So Uncle Harry's punishment is inconsistent because it will be related more to his frustrations and moods than to the mistakes. If Dad or Mom use Harry's idea when they have had it "up to here," Nancy and Martin will be more interested in that frustration point as their signal to ease up just short of the boiling points of Mom and Dad.

Reason #3:
Punishment will be Imitated

We usually think of a child's or teen's imitation of parents as very specific. *"Look at the way he walks, just like his Dad."* *"Look at the way she does her hair, trying to be just like Mom."* But copying Mom and Dad is more likely to involve social habits. How does Mom handle situations when things don't go right? What is her solution when others don't do what she wants? If Dad gets frustrated, how does he react?

> *Kids can get the message that the punishment used by Mom and Dad is a good way to deal with people.*

We all know how quickly kids will pick up those words of frustration when Dad hits himself on the kitchen drawer, but they also pick up the cues on *how to react* when things go wrong. Kids can get the message that the punishment used by Mom and Dad is a good way to deal with people.

The imitation of punishment will be included in the rest of the teen's social life. How should he handle friends when they don't do the "right thing?" The parent becomes a role model for punishment. *"It works for Mom, maybe it will work for me when I feel like it."* In any case, the most natural reflex to punishment is to give some back. If it is not possible to punish the parent, the teen will turn to others.

> *The goal of teaching how to react to others may be more important than correcting the mistake itself.*

So there's the possibility that your teen will pick up some cues from your behavior about what the appropriate reaction to unwanted behavior is. If a daughter frequently criticizes and yells at her baby brother, a careful observation of the parents' own reactions might be a clue as to where the daughter's reactions come from.

Children make a lot of mistakes, being led into errors by peers, forgetting chores and commitments, indulging in unhealthy foods, and wasting time, to mention a few. **When parents see so many errors, they may find it difficult to be accepting and look at the long run. But the goal of teaching how to react to others may be more important than correcting the mistake itself!**

Reason #4:
Punishment is Insulting, Belittling, and Lowers a Person's Self -Esteem

The emotional put-down of punishment distracts the person from learning about the desired behavior. The punishment act, itself, is childish and belittles the significance and power of the person who is punished. **Isn't that why *adults* are so insulted when punishment is tried on them?** We all know the only possibly appropriate ages for punishment are from 2 to 18.

Once the child's or teen's value of himself goes down and the fear starts up, a new disadvantage develops for learning. Much of childhood is a trial-and-error process. The discoveries of how to get along come from a lot of guesses. How much guessing will a frightened person risk? Once the teen becomes discouraged and engaged in self-degrading thoughts, parents and teachers know learning will be slow.

In my college course in animal learning, students had to teach their own pigeon to perform tasks by rewarding small successes. The first task was to get the pigeon to peck a disc by first rewarding it with seeds for stepping toward the disc, followed by putting its head toward it, then touching, and then pecking.

Sometimes students had trouble with the project because their pigeon was too scared to even move in its cage. If it had been handled roughly or it had escaped and been chased down before being put in the learning cage, it was too upset to do anything! Pigeons that won't do anything can't be taught anything! The student stares at the pigeon waiting for a chance to reward success. The pigeon stares at the student waiting for a chance to get out!

Punishment can produce the same impasse between a teen and a parent.

Reason #5:
Punishment Encourages Stressful Behaviors

Punishment will encourage bad habits such as nail-biting, hair-twirling, and *"safer obsessions"* like video games and TV. These *"escapes"* are very stubborn habits maintained by their usefulness for avoiding contact with the punisher. Whenever encouragement and reward are low, these stress behaviors will increase. If the stressful behavior attracts some parental attention, then we are in a vicious cycle with a new long-term problem.

Reason #6:
The Power Struggle

Punishment will tempt the teen to resist the parent's intimid-ation; the struggle takes over the family airways leaving little time for positive interactions and learning. The parent can "win" the power struggle, but **for every winner a loser is made!**

The power struggle of punishment can spread to all family members. As others pick up the habit, a competition develops, *"Who can 'outdo'* (put down, criticize, reprimand, catch more mistakes of) *whom???"* It ruins the family as a nurturing place where learning is encouraged through practice—*with* mistakes.

Reason #7:
It's a Short-term Trap That Can Last Forever!

The *parental* bad habit of using punishment can be stubborn because it produces short-term results. For example, when Martin aggravates his Aunt Hazel, she may keep him in line by finding fault where he is vulnerable, *"That music is terrible. Your hair is a mess! Your face is breaking out again."*

With each of the insults, Martin's obnoxious behavior is temporarily interrupted while he defends himself, Hazel has released a little tension, and maybe Hazel has "taught Martin a lesson" or at least evened the score.

The long-term disadvantages of Hazel's punishment habit may go undetected because they will grow slowly. Martin will start the bad escape habits, he will feel worse about himself and about Aunt Hazel, and *he* will try to use punishment himself to "get even."

These two people are well on the way to a poor relationship where Martin annoys Aunt Hazel just to get even and Aunt Hazel boils over now and then to gain temporary relief from her allergic reaction to him. Martin will learn when to let up a little, and he may also learn to imitate her insulting style just to gain more control.

Reason #8:
Discrimination

A teen subjected to a parent or relative in the *"I'll-get-even-with-you"* game learns the signals well. The innocent chaperones and teachers become fair game until they learn how to insult or scowl miserably enough to get control. An additional social problem is that no adult around a teen like Martin likes to be forced to act mad or abusive and would rather avoid him, because they don't like the person they must become to keep control.

The parent suffers most from the frequent punishment policy, and the teen may suffer less because he learns to adjust to people who will play his game and those who will not.

We all develop discriminations and act differently with different people. But when punishment is used, we do our best to avoid the punishing person altogether. **The negative, critical and threatening boss may have a reputation as a hard-liner, but the employees will duck and dodge her as much as possible.** And they'll give no extra effort. Who wants to please her?

The relationship that develops is one in which two people only barely tolerate each other because they are forced to. The teen would like to escape such a situation because of the possibility of being punished, and the parent would rather be away (at work, at meetings, or just out anywhere) because of the uncomfortable parental reactions that seem to be called for in the situation.

Reason #9:
Relatives Will Go Home,
Parents Will Be Left Behind

When Uncle Harry leaves, Mom and Dad are left with the long-term side effects of punishments that were too much for the teen—too severe, too frequent. The teen's solution may be to stop responding altogether or, at least, to respond as little as possible. The situation has produced a kind of success, the teen *is* quiet.

Even if the adults try a better approach later on, the teen may refuse to risk coming out of his or her shell. The biggest wish of this kid is to get out—out of the room, out of sight, out of the house, if possible. Wouldn't we all rather dodge the punishment? **With punishment you have to find your teen; with praise, your teen finds you.**

With repeated experience, the situation preceding punishment signals a need to withdraw. The signal could be a classroom, a house, a time of day, a particularly dangerous person, or a combination of these. Once experiences have taught these signals, the mere termination of punishment is not likely to be effective immediately, because your teen will be unwilling to take risks to find out if danger has passed.

> *With punishment,*
> *you have to find*
> *your teen;*
> *with praise,*
> *your teen finds you.*

Uncle Harry and Aunt Hazel will also leave behind other unintended effects. Activities and behaviors that explore new opportunities for learning may be reduced because they now seem dangerous or potentially embarrassing. **Often your opinion of your son or daughter is better understood than the specific reasons for punishment.** The details of why you are so angry are smothered in the emotion, fear, and desire to suppress the memory of the whole experience. The lack of understanding combines with the fear of risking any more punishment, and we are well on the way to stopping all progress in this situation.

Left on their own with Harry's punishment advice, parents will be tempted to increase the punishment when the kids don't seem to get the message. But punishment gives too little information anyway—it only tells you one of the things you ought *not* to do, nothing about what *to do*.

> *Punishment gives too little information. It only tells you one of the things you ought not to do, nothing about what to do.*

To reverse Uncle Harry's effects, a reduction in punishment must be accompanied with an increase in opportunities for genuine encouragement. Very minor events can act as punishments for a timid teen. Simply interrupting him at dinner may silence him for the whole meal. A verbal snap from his sibling may accomplish the same thing. It will require many isolated one-on-one moments with generous parents showing great tolerance and support to draw him out.

Many of Uncle Harry's threats will very likely be of the one-shot nature if his stay is longer than a day (perish the thought). As the punishments fail to produce results, he may opt for large punishments such as canceling a trip or party. Usually one-shots are too late and produce the most resentment and argument with the least amount of change. Since parties and trips are infrequent, he feels he has to threaten a lot just to milk as much influence as possible from the upcoming event. Once the party's over a new threat will have to be dreamed up, or, if Harry's gone, the parents will be left with that job.

The one-shot leaves the parents with the dreary task of sorting out threats, bluffs, and final conclusions. In the process they are likely to fall into a negative reinforcement habit.

Negative Reinforcement

Isn't negative reinforcement the same as punishment? No, it's more subtle but also more common. The purpose of regular punishment, as everyone knows, is to reduce or eliminate bad behavior. **Negative reinforcement is not punishment for mistakes, it's punishment for <u>failing</u> to do the right thing!** The threat of a consequence for failing to meet someone's expectations is a common experience in a routine day. Why do I make dinner for the kids at the same time every night, use their favorite plate, prepare only certain foods? Is it because they watch for their chance to support my "good" behavior? No, the answer here usually begins, *"Well, if I didn't do that, the kids would complain and make a lot of trouble."*

When it is the *lack* of performance that produces bad consequences, it's called negative reinforcement. As long as I avoid unwanted dinner plates, unwanted food, delays, and don't disappoint my little masters, *I avoid* their nasty behavior.

Parents also use negative reinforcement. For example, as long as the kids don't act up and fight, *they can avoid* my mad reaction.

The difference between regular punishment and negative reinforcement is important because the threat of negative reinforcement is always hounding you. It has a continuous nature to it and, if not tested, the fear can continue long after the threat is passed.

Regular punishment in its consistent form, even with all its faults, is easy to understand: *"If I do the wrong thing, I'll get bad consequences."* Negative reinforcement has all the same faults with the added confusion of an obscure rule: *"If I <u>fail</u> to do the right thing, I'll get bad consequences."*

Mom: *"Zac, did you pick up your clothes?"*

Zac: (Watching TV) *"Not yet."*

Mom: *"Did you put your dirty clothes in the laundry?"*

Zac: *"No."*

Mom: *"How about the mess in the living room?"*

Zac: *"OK. As soon as this is over."*

Mom: *"Take those dishes out, too."*

Zac: *"OK"* (Remains an intimate part of the couch.)

Mom: (She's used no punishment so far, but now she reacts to Zac's *lack* of action.) *"Zac, I have had it! Now turn off that TV and get these things cleaned up!"*

Zac: *"OK, OK, don't have a cow about it."* (Mumbling) *"Gee, who knows when you're gonna blow up, anyway?"*

Mom: *"What was that?"*

Zac: *"Nothing."*

Part of Zac's and Mom's problem is that Mom's strategy is the use of negative reinforcement. If Zac fails to perform (enough times) and Mom asks him (enough times) then Mom gets mad. Mom may also support and compliment Zac if he cleans things up, but Mom's exasperation limit and Zac's fear of her are the main factors at work in the situation.

At times, the distinction between regular punishment and negative reinforcement may seem like a word game. Could we simply say that Mom threatens regular punishment for Zac's sloppiness? She *could* use that strategy—dock his allowance when he leaves his clothes all over, for example. But her reaction is negative reinforcement because it is triggered by the *lack* of behaviors and occurs at a non-specific time. Zac is tempted to continue to procrastinate, delay, and test the limits while Mom is driven to using "mad" as a motivator.

Negative reinforcement does not produce a happy situation. If you do most of your activities everyday just to avoid someone's flack, you're probably unhappy with him or her (all spouses know who I'm talking about). *Positive* reinforcement is needed for a good relationship.

> Dad: *"Did you take the car in today?"*
> Mom: *"Yes, it just needed a tune up."*
> Dad: *"Great, thanks for getting it over there; that takes a lot off my mind."*

Dad used the positive reinforcement idea, but in the next minute he slips to negative reinforcement:

> Dad: *"Did you get the little dinners I wanted for lunches?"*
> Mom: *"Didn't go by the store after work."*
> Dad: *"Hey, how am I supposed to work all day without lunch?"* (Here's a reprimand as negative reinforcement for Mom's failure to do the right thing.)
> Mom: (Borrowing from Zac) *"OK, OK, don't have a cow over it. I'll get them tomorrow and I'll make something good for you to take in the morning."* (Mumbling) *"Gee, beam me up, Scotty!"*
> Dad: *"What was that?"*
> Mom: *"Nothing."*

Negative reinforcement in combination with an upcoming, one-shot event is a tempting strategy to try to get the kids to do right. *"If you don't stop complaining all the time, we'll just give up going to the beach this summer."* or, *"You had better show me you can get along with your brother or I won't sign you up for soccer this year."* Because the threatened events happen only once or, at most, once a year, they can't be a part of *repeated* practice—unless we add a lot of nagging, *"Remember what I said, treat your brother nice or no soccer!"*

The threats for not acting right sound a lot like negative reinforcement with all its bad baggage, so nagging sets in to try to use the one-shot event to get a little cooperation now.

Going to the beach is a singular future event not likely to be repeated for some time. It's tempting to repeat the *threat* many times since the vacation itself will only happen once. It's true that your teen needs to learn that you should be taken seriously and that you mean what you say about the beach or about soccer, but the consequence is so far off that any outcome will seem arbitrary.

So after all the argument, you either take the kid to the beach anyway, or you hold to your threat and don't take her/him. The first choice seems too lenient, but the second is too tough because it says that overall, he/she has been a bad kid. This one-shot consequence has no winners and little chance of a satisfactory outcome.

This situation is gloomy for the family and for the event when it finally comes. It's like holding off the enemy in battle with only one bullet; you have to do a lot of posturing, bluffing, and threatening. Once you use your bullet, you are an ogre for not allowing the beach or soccer or you are a patsy for giving in! **And then the next day, you will need a new bullet and a new threat.**

A better strategy is to allow yourself and your family the enjoyment of individual events without trying to use them to limit bad behavior or produce good behavior. Instead, choose some smaller event that can come up more frequently, something not so severe that has a positive side to emphasize. For example,

instead of threatening to ground your teen next semester if grades
don't come up (an unmanageable threat with an "only once"
character to it), possibly each good grade on any test, quiz or paper
could produce a guaranteed 2 weeks of regular "going out"
privileges. This procedure has the advantage of being a consistent
and repeatable consequence while the parent emphasizes the right
habits. It is not negative or severe, so the parents don't need to feel
guilty and inconsistent. Also, it is logically related to the need for
study time.

**A very repeatable consequence makes it much easier to
refrain from nagging. The repetition does the reminding.**
Nagging on the problem can stop, and the airways can be opened
up for more pleasant family talk.

Reason # 10:
Small Punishments Can Lead to the Ultimate Punishment— Divorce of Parent from Teen.

Any person being punished has one thought in mind, *"Get
away!"* Teens could plan running away or withdrawing if running
away is impractical. And yet the conflict and confusion are
intensified because your home is their most important source of
security.

So don't talk about divorcing your children. This ultimate consequence is too disturbing and implies that your love for your teen
can be easily traded away. Your love and loyalty should have a
higher price tag and not become part of bluffing or bargaining.

Whenever punishment is used, the parent is counting on some
other aspect of the situation to keep the teen within range for
deserved punishments. Either the doors must be locked, literally or
figuratively, or the rewards from the parents are enough to

overwhelm the unhappiness. **No matter how effective punitive measures may seem in the short-run, the parents risk losing their teen. That's why these strategies usually don't work on adults—adults can leave.**

So Why Would Anyone Use Punishment?

With all these discouraging problems, you might wonder why some parents continue to use punishment. Even parent behavior should diminish when it is unsuccessful. So when their action (punishment) doesn't get the desired result, why don't they just quit?

The answer is that in the very short term, punishment produces some results. If Mom punishes Fred for using bad language by grounding him, Mom's punishment is reinforced by its immediate effect in interrupting Fred's bad behavior temporarily.

Parents, particularly American parents, hurried by schedules filled with job and family responsibilities, often hope for the "quick-fix." Punishment may seem to fill the bill, but the disadvantages far outweigh the advantage of a temporary effect. That's why we use it so seldom on adults. Instead, we use the alternatives of the next chapter.

STEP 8
Use Alternatives to Punishment

(What is a Good *Adult* "Get Tough Policy?)

A large investment firm reneged on a $1.3 million dividend last year because an accountant left off the minus sign—it was really a $1.3 million *shortfall!* How did the firm's president discipline his accountant for the $2.6 million mistake? To his disappointed stockholders he said, *"I guess that's why they put erasers on pencils!* With adults, we usually get on with fixing the mistake. We deal with unwanted adult behavior every day, but most of us gave up punishment of the straightforward kind long ago. The culture we live in continues to provide some punishment—"logical consequences" we sometimes call them—and the courts hand out punishments for the larger transgressions. But logical consequences and court sentences are usually long delayed and given only for repeated bad habits and big mistakes. So with

> *We all deal with unwanted adult behavior every day, but most of us gave up punishment of the straightforward kind long ago.*

unwanted *adult* behavior what alternatives do we use?

Every day, adult mistakes receive *very kind* reactions. Even blowing your horn in traffic is considered too aggressive. Often we just allow the person to make amends, or we ignore the mistake altogether. If we control the situation, we might try to make it less likely he will repeat the mistake: *"The boss should give better instructions. He should put up more signs about how to use the printer!"* After more instruction, the boss may use warnings: *"Anyone caught putting their sandwich in the printer will be ..."* Then, if that doesn't work, maybe, punishment.

Along with *making amends*, we'll also take up the pros and cons of *ignoring*, adding a *guarantee for good behavior, changing the convenience* and *using "count-outs and time-outs."*

Since punishment has so many disadvantages anyway, let's get on to a more adult way of handling problems.

Alternative #1: Making Amends

Making amends is the number one strategy adults use to handle bad adult behavior.

> *You expect to be allowed to make amends; you expect me to belittle the problem, you even expect sympathy.*

If you come to my house for dinner tonight and spill your drink at the table, you don't expect me to say: *"Hey! What do you think you're doing? You're so clumsy! Now pay attention to what you're doing, or I'll send you home!"*

What nerve! Treating a guest like a child. What happened to "the benefit of the doubt?" You expect to be allowed to make amends; you expect me to belittle the problem, you even expect sympathy. *"Oh, too bad. No problem, I'll get a cloth."* You say, *"I'm sorry, let me get that. I'll take care of it."*

Isn't adulthood nice? Even with big mistakes, we would rather have the offender try to fix the mistake than punish him. At what age did you, and our innocent accountant with the 2.6 billion dollar mistake, earn such consideration? Why wasn't *he* punished? Because it would look as if the investment firm was a simple-minded company, naive and heartless. After all, mistakes happen.

Two-year-olds, teenagers, or accountants who make mistakes, accidental or not, should be allowed to make amends. Not that the accountant is likely to make up his mistake in this century. Your teen deserves the same respect. It is only fair to assume he or she is doing his or her best.

Remember the movie about a troublesome city teen whose life was popping with mistakes that he could never see coming. His parents punished him, hoping he would avoid future "accidents." At last, in exasperation they sent him to the country to live with relatives. We saw the teen toil the whole afternoon cleaning up a clumsy mistake before supper—making amends. Finally finished, he went into dinner, justified, uncriticized, and with an experience that motivated him to be more careful.

At home he would have been restricted or physically punished and belittled, and he would have lost practice at making things right. Though the movie lesson was unrealistically easy and quick, the message was a good one: the teen learned by making amends and cleared up his guilt; the adults maintained a healthier relationship with the teen in the bargain.

> Grandma: (Sitting down to dinner) *"Whoops, now I know what I forgot at the store—coffee! But we have juice, how about that?"*
>
> Mom: *"Don't worry about it; juice is fine. We'll get the coffee tomorrow."* (Mom belittles mistake)

Grandma: *"At least I'll get out the juice."* (Grandma makes Amends)

Nancy: *"I accidentally erased our list of names and addresses from the computer today."*

Grandma: *"What! Didn't you put it back from an old disc? I was looking for that for half an hour this afternoon. You're so inconsiderate at times. Don't you have enough sense to..."*

Mom: (Interrupting) *"Nancy, after dinner, find the old disc and reload the address file, OK?"* (And then to Grandma) *"I can get along without the coffee until tomorrow if you can, so don't you worry about it."*

Grandma: *"What? Oh, ah, yes, OK, OK. If I get a break on forgetting the coffee, I guess Nancy gets a break, too. And, Nancy, could you add the names on the outside of my phone book?"*

Alternative #2: Ignoring

Ignoring bad behavior eventually decreases it, especially if your teen was acting up to get attention. If a parent can tough it out and hold back attention for the bad behavior, the teen may go on to something else. The problem here is that in the short-run, *more bad behavior* is likely rather than less. This bad behavior has been a part of a habit to get some entertainment, or attention from Mom and Dad. Now the parents plan to cut that off. For example, no more attention for bad language.

If the usual amount of swearing will no longer work, their teen may escalate the volume, frequency, or foulness of the talk. At the "higher" level, the parents may break the new rule and punish this outrageous behavior. If that quiets things down, the parents may return to the ignoring rule only to go back to punishment when the assault on the ears again reaches pain threshold. The process builds up a new level of bad behavior. **Escalation is a very common problem because the natural childish ("teenish?") reaction to failure (to get attention) is escalation.**

Ignoring means consistently overlooking relatively unimportant, undesirable behaviors and paying attention to other aspects of a teen's actions. When Tim shaved the hair around his ears, his parents felt it was within his personal grooming choices to do so, but when he slapped his younger sister, they reacted strongly. Their different reactions to these very different behaviors keep the priorities straight and reduce unnecessary criticism.

When you react to a behavior of your teen, keep the overall family atmosphere in mind. Sacrifice family atmosphere only when necessary. In Exercise 4 you listed unwanted behaviors and rank ordered them. If an action takes a low priority rating, it doesn't deserve your time and energy, nor a lot of family disruption.

You may want to ignore behaviors that occur only occasionally as well as others that come under the teen's growing sphere of control, for example: keeping a messy bedroom, using poor grammar, wearing strange outfits and unusual hairstyles. The parents' greatest influences on these daily habits will not be by way of arguments and consequences, but the model they present. Some behaviors are part of passing stages that will be outgrown, and therefore they are easier to ignore. When your teen invites a friend to visit, the bedroom will be spruced up to *their* level of tolerance. Unwanted grammar, language, clothing, and hairstyles are probably temporary, fluctuating with peer and media influences.

One 13-year-old sprayed her hair to stand up six inches above her forehead and wore glaring makeup, but she was a good student with pleasant social skills. It was a tribute to her parents' ability to overlook extremes of grooming and focus instead on her *important* actions. Extremes of personal care will probably change toward the norm when the teenager wants to fit into a different group or workplace.

Alternative #3:
Adding Something Good to the Ignoring Plan

Mom and Dad need to have a plan to encourage good behaviors and be alert to the first opportunity to work the plan! Ignoring the unwanted behavior *and* planning to encourage *specific, likely,* good behaviors will produce better results. The message needs to be clear: *"Now that's a good way to handle that." "I liked hearing about your report on the Civil War battle. You're learning about interesting things." "I noticed you helped clear the table after supper. That was great!"*

> *Ignoring the unwanted behavior and planning to encourage specific, likely, good behaviors will produce better results.*

"Catch 'em Being Good" means recognize, praise, or reward the good behavior you see.

Perhaps you remember as a child thinking, *"When I make mistakes everyone notices and I get in trouble, but a lot of times I do well, and nobody ever says a thing."*

To prevent unwanted behaviors, parents need to "catch 'em being good," not just when the desired behavior occurs, but when a behavior in the right direction comes along. Actions that are improvements and steps forward need the most encouragement, recognition, praise, and reward.

Research tells us that catching people when they come near to appropriate behavior is a more efficient learning technique than punishment for errors. Considering all the possibilities for error, a teen isn't much closer to learning an important skill just by being told, *"Wrong!"*

Which choice is more likely to produce positive results?

1. Teen has no friends. You can:
   a) discuss the importance of having friends, or
   b) listen and encourage any socializing in the family and outside it.
2. This young adult pouts and sulks. Would you:
   a) tell him to stop being so sour when it's not justified?
   b) ignore pouting and talk pleasantly when the teen is sociable?
3. He/she has no outside interests. You can:
   a) require the teen to choose two activities of his/her choice and insist on participation for a half-year, or
   b) you can be available to listen for his/her interests. When the teen wants to participate in an activity, provide transportation.

In the first example, discussing friendship will be pointedly painful to the teen, but listening and socializing in the family will provide practice and build confidence for the teen to reach out in other situations.

In example two, reactions of anger to pouting will give attention to poor behavior and possibly encourage it with an argument about its justification. The better plan is to support the less frequent, appropriate, pleasant interactions.

In the third case about outside interests, both choices are helpful and correct for a teen who needs to develop activities.

Insisting on some selections takes authority, but that may be an ingredient needed to get things started.

Alternative #4:
Using the Cost of Inconvenience

Many little inconveniences, particularly those for teens and adults, may seem at first trivial, but when put into practice they may be extremely effective. For example, if Dad has to put a penny in a jar on the kitchen table every time he loses his temper, it may seem like a trivial act for someone with plenty of pennies. But if the rule is strictly followed, the inconvenience of having to stop, get a penny, and go into the kitchen and put it in the jar can be a very effective consequence. **It's not the money but the behavioral "cost" that makes this consequence work.**

Many psychologists use the principle of inconvenience as a strategy for removing or reducing smoking in adults. The heavy smoker is instructed to keep an exact record of his smoking throughout each day. He carries a little notebook wherever he goes and writes down the time, to the minute, when he takes out a cigarette, and the time he puts it out. He may be asked to note the situation as well, including who was with him and what he was doing. Some psychologists also ask for the cigarette butts to be saved and brought in for counting. These tasks may not seem like consequences as we have talked about them so far, but they are consequences of a most useful type. They are costly in time and **many a smoker is just too busy to make all those entries and save butts, so he takes a pass on having that cigarette.**

Such a self-administered procedure requires a very cooperative and trustworthy subject. I have found the cost-of-inconvenience

> *Inconvenience can be a very effective consequence.*

procedure useful with smokers referred to me who have been told by their doctor that their health or even their life is at stake! They usually *want* the process to work, and they can be counted on to try hard. The procedure has not worked well when used on people who *"feel they should cut down"* or quit for the children's sake. With these less motivated subjects, it takes a stronger procedure than raising the cost of inconvenience.

Sometimes children can be enthusiastic about a record-keeping procedure. One mother reported that her 19-year-old son, Damon, continually disrupted the family by "checking things." On some evenings, he insisted on checking as many as 70 things before going to sleep. Damon checked to see if the back door was locked. He checked to see if the light was out in the basement. He checked to see if his pen was on his desk, and if his dresser drawers were closed. Some of this would have been reasonable, but the situation got out of hand when he checked the same thing for the fifth or sixth time in the same evening!

At first his checking was examined for the possibility that it was an attention-getting behavior. Some progress was made by reducing Damon's parents' attention to the excessive checking and increasing conversation time before he went off to bed. The most effective procedure was beginning a record of every item checked, the time it was checked, the result of the check, and what could have happened if the item had been left unchecked. The procedure involved so much writing and decision-making that it was nearly impossible to check 70 things each evening.

Because of the work and inconvenience of the procedure, Damon began to pass up items that were not so important, and he made a special effort to remember the ones already checked, or look at his record, so that he didn't have to do it again! The number of times Damon checked things soon was down to a level that was only a little unusual instead of disruptive to the family.

The same principle of inconvenience can be used to increase a habit. For example, good homework habits can be influenced by how convenient it is to get started. If there is a place to do homework with little distraction that is well supplied with paper and such, then we have a better chance of getting some homework done.

> Dianne: *"I'm not going to practice this stupid violin any more, it's too much trouble!"*
>
> Mom: *"Just another ten minutes, then you can quit."*
>
> Dianne: *"Phooey."*

Dianne's practice is best done in intervals that keep frustration to a minimum, but once Dianne begins, Mom hates to let her quit because it's such a hassle to get her to start again. **Maybe Mom could do away with some inconveniences associated with Dianne's "re-starts."** She could help Dianne get out the music, set up the stand. Then while Dianne checks the tuning, Mom could turn off the TV and get everyone else far enough away. If some of these inconveniences could be done away with, maybe Dianne would practice more frequently.

> Mom: *"Let's set up a special place for you. How about in our bedroom? We're never in there when you need to practice and it's away from the TV and your brother. You can leave your music and stand out, and it won't be disturbed."*
>
> Dianne: *"OK, but I still think all this practice is stupid."*

We have not solved the violin problem by just finding a place for practice. Dianne is going to need more encouragement than that. Mom needs to visit the practice situation a lot, comment on

Dianne's progress, and help the instructor find practice pieces that interest Dianne. But **a place to practice easily, without frustrating start-up time, is a step toward making good practice convenient.**

Alternative #5:
Direct Consequences, Even Count-outs and Time-outs, Must Give Way to Modeling

Sometimes the bad behavior demands a reaction. We don't let adults get away with just anything and teens becoming adults shouldn't be misled that anything goes either. What alternative is there when bad behavior should not be ignored and making amends or hoping for opportunities for encouragement is not enough?

For young children, time-out is often a good solution but may not be appropriate for teens—especially older teens. We all know the drill of putting the child on a chair or in his/her room for a little "cooling off" and isolation as a kind of punishment. The procedure can work well if the threats, arguments, and other verbal decorations that often precede the time-out can be kept to a minimum.

Mom:	(Liz throws a toy at her sister.) *"Liz! We don't throw toys. You could hurt someone. That's One!"* (Liz throws again.) *"Liz, I told you, that's Two"*
Liz:	*"I don't want it!"* (Liz throws again.)
Mom:	*"OK, that's Three,"* Mom takes Liz to the kitchen chair and deposits her there.

Mom is doing well with her younger one. She doesn't talk much during the count which could lead Liz to act up more, **she doesn't make a lot of threats, and she corrects the behavior in a way that can be used frequently—no dramatic punishment that requires a big build-up.**

Time-out for young teens means spending a short time in a quiet place, alone, after inappropriate behavior. It can be very successful. The separation of younger teens from others interrupts overheated verbal and physical reactions with a calming-down period. When the teen has regained emotional control she or he can discuss what happened and plan changes. The time period that is most helpful is long enough to break up unwanted behavior and tempers, but short enough for everyone to remember clearly what happened and to want to plan other reactions. Just having time-out for a minute or two is effective; a long time-out is not necessary.

This alternative cuts off fighting between siblings and helps a parent regain perspective and control, instead of escalating a problem situation. Parents who try time-out find it prevents them from using physical and verbal punishments they regret later.

When parents react with punishments they frequently prevent discussion and planning for changes. Because of bad feelings, the bad behavior may occur again. But after time-out, each person involved in the problem has a chance to tell his/her feelings and make suggestions. The parent and teen can practice the listening and understanding of Step 1, and gain experience planning for a change. Time-out sets the stage for a new beginning.

When Mom returned from shopping, she noticed lipstick on the kitchen wall. Mike had been talking on the phone instead of watching his younger sister, Tina, the wall artist.

Mike: *"But I have to talk on the phone to my friends*
            sometimes. It drives me crazy to watch Tina

	every minute. I shouldn't have to watch her this much! How could she do that? Mom, you've raised her all wrong. I'm not going to clean that up. I have to leave to go to the mall with Bill."
Mom:	*"We're going to have to talk about this."*
Mike:	*"I can't stand it! It's not my fault, and Tina should have to clean it up! Mom, you can't make me do this."*
Mom:	*"Mike, I'm getting mad and you're upset too. Cool off for five minutes in your room, and then we'll put our heads together to work this out."* (Mike stomps out to his room.)

When the two get together after cooling down, it's more likely they will be able to make a compromise. Perhaps Mom, Mike, and Tina can do the wall cleaning together. The baby-sitting needs more planning and incentives. Mike needs some specific activities to do with Tina while baby-sitting, and he can be given extra time with his friends for doing a good job. When you try to reach a solution, if either you or your teen find you can't be reasonable, extend the time-out until all persons can contribute to the agreement.

Dad was proud of his intelligent son and daughters, but when the girls fought, he couldn't tolerate it. Joy and Bonnie started kidding around and then sparring in the upstairs hall. When a framed picture hit the floor, Dad ran to the stairway and shouted for them to stop, *"Joy and Bonnie, you go to your rooms and we'll discuss this in 15 minutes if you're ready to talk reasonably!"*

Dad's girls are almost adults; it's time for them to find ways to keep their playfulness from escalating to breaking up the house. Dad's discussion with them as near-equals may help them share responsibility for controlling themselves as they reach for adulthood.

For a teen who is almost an adult, the time-out method will seem more and more childish. After all, you seldom see it used in the adult world. Your example, on the other hand, will always be an influence on your teen's behavior even in the decades to come.

Both parent modeling and family identification help a young person keep direction. Mom said, *"In the Weiler family we try to think of and respect everyone in the family and outside of it. I expect you to live up to the Weiler standard."* Of course Mom's actions must follow her words. Family sayings get across things the parents consider important. A father was fond of saying, *"With all thy getting, get understanding."*

> *Speaking and acting in ways that show consideration for our teens' needs and capabilities will produce respect in return.*

The following examples show how modeling and positive consequences work together. A parent who wanted a teen to read books turned off the TV and began reading an exciting adventure novel aloud with her teen. A mother who wants her daughter to be honest can ask, *"Whose money is this under the kitchen table?"* instead of just pocketing it. When a father noticed shoes accumulating by the front door, he put his in the closet, and soon the teen's were not there either. The power of what we do is surprising; it's natural for members of the family to observe and be affected by it. Imitation occurs every day.

A teen developed a problem controlling anger. He started fights when classmates teased him and felt bad about himself later. His parents needed to demonstrate and describe their methods of controlling anger in their lives. Mom shared a story: *"I was driving to the post office today and when I changed lanes, another driver honked a long time at me. I guess he thought I slowed him down. I felt mad and thought about pulling over and shaking my fist at him. But I said to myself, 'I'm angry, but I'm in control— not him. I'm not going to let him make me do something dangerous.'"* Sharing family experiences is an important part of modeling.

Try this modeling exercise. Bring family members together to make lists of each other's actions. Each person writes everyone's name, including his/her own, on a piece of paper. Ask each person to list the most positive action of each member of the family after each name. Which persons work hard? Which ones have the most interesting stories, are creative, dress fashionably, use good manners, tell jokes or funny stories? Add actions that come to mind, but keep them on the positive side. This is not a gripe session.

After everyone has written a list, exchange sheets and ask someone to tell one of the answers on the sheet. Talk over these answers briefly but move right along to the next person and answer. The idea is to have people think about the positive actions of the ones they live with and encourage these activities.

The last part of this exercise is a discussion in which people pretend they are other members of the family. Let people choose their roles, and everyone can guess who is who as the discussion goes along. Select a discussion topic such as, where should we go on the next family outing? The purpose is merely to see how alike we are and yet how we each have a different view of others. Also, we may gain a clearer understanding of how much of our person- alities are a function of those we live with.

The Work of Being a Parent

Allowing a teen to make amends, using time-outs, ignoring some things, looking for something good, and watching your own example, *all* require diligent effort. Contrary to the easy magical advice from aunts, uncles, or some professionals, being a parent can be downright hard work. So make sure you eliminate rules about trivial behaviors before you start any of these plans. Here's an exercise to start the habit of keeping the rules appropriate and on target.

Exercise 9 (Taking On a Few Good Rules)
A Planning Session Agenda

Planning sessions have a dangerous tendency to turn into general gripe sessions. Although complaining can be therapeutic for parents, they often jump around from one problem to another without concluding a plan for any particular problem.

So a planning session needs an agenda that determines parental reactions to a particular situation. The session should also produce an overall understanding of what is going on when the specific problem is encountered.

The purpose of this exercise is to do a complete "walk through" of a problem you identified in the earlier exercises. You may not always need such a complete analysis, but for the purpose of becoming alert to the possible aspects of behavior, this exercise will include all the steps.

First select a behavior from your priority list at the end of Exercise 4. This will be the problem under discussion in this session.

The Behavior Chart

Create a three-day chart that shows specific behaviors, punishments, and alternatives you could use. As you fill in your chart, think of the behavior you want. What would you have done if the wanted behavior had occurred instead of the unwanted action? Would you have reacted positively just as you reacted negatively to the error? Was any part of the desired behavior done before the mistakes were made? If so, what encouragement did you give? This chart will be helpful when talking over a behavior with your teen. A sample chart follows on the next page.

A: Fill out a Behavior Chart. A short outline of the chart is presented below. You will not yet have a record of the behavior as described in the last part of the chart, but you can put down your own observations as you remember them to answer those questions.

A Sample Behavior Chart

Day	Unwanted Behavior	Punishment or Other Negative Reaction	Behavior You Want	Positive Reaction, Making Amends, or Other "Reward"
Sat. 10 am	Left house before doing chores	Criticized; given chores, extra work, grounded	Do chores before leaving;	Discuss plan and incentives, provide extra on allowance
Sat. 10 pm	Curfew violated	Reprimanded; grounded; no phone use.	Be on time; call early next time	Discuss curfew; come in extra early next time.
Sun. 2 pm	Homework not done	Criticized; can't see TV or friends	Complete homework; spend 1 extra hour studying	Discuss plan of homework; discuss incentives and value of topics
Mon. 5 pm	Fighting; made hole in bedroom wall	Reprimanded and sent to room; no TV	Talk ; no horsing around in house	Talk over problem; fix hole together

As you fill in the chart, ask yourself these questions:

1: What is an objective description of the behavior?

2: What happened next?

3: Where would you place the possible blames and/or credits?

4: At what age would you expect an average teen to do what you are hoping will be done in this situation?

5: How could you allow more practice?

6: When do things happen? (keep record)

B: Review this check list for consequences as you consider possible reactions to the behavior. Pose each of the following questions in the planning session:

1. **Is the problem big enough to bother with?** Remember even a "No" here should indicate a strategy—a strategy to eliminate nagging your teen or yourself about the problem.

2. **Am I attempting too much at one time?** A tempting pitfall in parenting is to try too many changes at once. Don't attempt to control eating, piano practicing, bed-making, and homework all at once. Concentrating on too many plans leads to mistakes and too much "policing." Think small. Begin with one rule at a time.

3. **Can the behavior be guaranteed without the management of consequences?** Some behaviors can be made impossible by engineering the environment and that strategy is sometimes easier than using rules. For example, a special kitchen drawer of utensils for a son or daughter's cooking projects may be easier than worrying about accidents with dangerous or fragile instruments.

4. **Have we thought of all the consequences that could be maintaining the behavior?** A good way to separate consequences is to consider what we have now? What usually happens when the "bad" behavior occurs and what happens next? What usually happens if she performs correctly? If we select a new consequence, how should we set up the practice?

5. **Is the consequence a one-shot?** In the one-shot consequence, a rule that can only work once, a parent uses a promise of something good or threat of something bad in the *future* as a consequence for a *present* behavior problem. Whichever way the consequence is stated, threat or promise, it has the same disagreeable characteristics: it is not repeatable, it tempts the parents to use repeated threats and will probably be somewhat arbitrary in the end. And then the next day what shall we do? Start a new threat?

6. **Is the consequence too severe?** Be sure that your selection of a consequence is not a reaction to one case of bad behavior. You want something that can be used repeatedly. As a matter of fact, the real test will come after things have settled down. The main feature of your plan that will help you through this test will be that you have planned to reward good behaviors reasonably and react to bad ones reasonably. So don't make plans when you're still angry over a mistake.

7. **If ignoring is the plan, are we prepared to handle the resulting escalation of the bad behavior? And what good behavior will we give attention to?**

8. **Is the expectation reasonable?** Your expectation may be reasonable but still much more than your daughter has ordinarily been doing. She was cleaning her room and now you want her to vacuum and dust the house. Remember we need to start where *she* is, not where you *wish* her to be.

9. **Is the consequence too weak?** What can be done if your teen just doesn't seem to care about the new consequence? It could be that you are not sticking to the rule and he really doesn't *have* to care. Or possibly he has too many freebies available or too many alternatives (If I can't go out, I'll watch TV!).

Are you starting with a behavior simple enough so that rewards can occur—even on the first day?

C: Review this Check List for Alternatives to Punishment.

1. Could you use the adult reaction to adult mistakes, *making amends?*
2. Is it possible to first try *ignoring?*
3. Could we help him or her to see us as a *good model.*
4. Have the other possibilities presented in this step been considered: *"Catch 'em being good,"* changing the *convenience* of the behavior, and *"Time-outs."*

Caring for Yourself in the Parenting Job.

STEP 9
Protect Your Feelings and Your Rights: Tolerate No Abuse!

Most parents are willing to give whatever effort is needed to produce good results. But usually they give very little consideration to their own comfort and welfare in the child/teen rearing process. This is a serious oversight. Raising a teen is a long process, and parents need to be as comfortable with it as possible.

Also, what the parents are willing to take will become a tolerance level that their teen is likely to acquire through imitation. Many mothers hope their daughters and sons will stick up for themselves in their occupation, marriage, and the sexist world they enter. And many regret some moments of over-reaction and hope for more thoughtful reactions from their own children. So now, for the benefit of both you *and* your teen, let's consider how raising an adult should come out *for you!*

Who Is Responsible?

Teenage cries for help often include accusations that the parents are to blame for whatever the teen is or does. Of course, parents do carry some responsibility, but their offspring will have to take responsibility for *themselves* if they are to grow up.

Even on the trivial side, these accusations should not go unchallenged because they prolong the childhood that now must be left behind: *"Mom, the car won't start!" "Dad, where are my shoes? I'm late!"* In trying to help with car trouble and lost shoes while meeting work demands, Mom and Dad often overlook their own feelings and rights.

The parent who continually accepts responsibility and blame and feels accountable for whatever goes wrong, sacrifices his/her own self-esteem. Although it is contradictory to do so, the teen may model the parent's sacrificial and self-deprecating disposition and at the same time be disappointed in the parent. Teens want to copy someone and the parent, right or wrong, is the most likely person. So teenagers may crave people who provide unreasonable sacrifices for them, and yet need parents to set an example that's better than that—an example where parents protect their own feelings and rights while balancing family and work loyalties.

> *When parents take care of their own needs, they help their teens as well as themselves.*

Growing teens can learn to apply a healthy adjustment to life's demands and joys if they live with a parent who exemplifies self-respect as well as helpfulness. When parents take care of their own needs, they help their teens as well as themselves.

Nine Parent Rights

Parents have the right to react when they are not treated with respect, and to say *"no"* when their rights and values are threatened. At times when efforts are not appreciated and interactions have soured, moms and dads have the right to express their feelings, think over choices, and change their minds. Parents have the right to make mistakes and still feel good about themselves.

These statements may seem too basic to be emphasized, but many parents need to be reminded of their own right to being less than perfect. It is unfair to hold a person to a standard of perfection—parent *or* teen. With the standard of perfection excluded, one feels a greater freedom to go ahead and try new solutions. Mistakes become evidence of trying

> *It is unfair to hold a person to a standard of perfection— parent or teen.*

some solution, not evidence of failure. *Both* parent and teen will find more solutions if their right to make mistakes is respected.

Many of the rights discussed here were first described in *The Assertive Option: Your Rights and responsibilities* by Patricia Jakubowski and Arthur J. Lange,* plus one or two variations I have added. Using these rights will provide a feeling of satisfaction with yourself and your family and preserve your spirit through your teen's growing-up years.

1) You have the right to your own values.

How much time do you want to put toward cleaning your car? Car care may have low priority on your list, and you may have to take some heat from family members who want a cleaner vehicle, less filled with "junk."

Parents have the right to spend time in ways that promote their own values, their own view of the important things in life, as long as others' rights are not hurt. So complaints about the poor condition of the car can trigger a plan for a future family activity but need not make you feel guilty.

---

* *The Assertive Option: Your Rights and Responsibilities* (pp.80-81) by P. Jakubowski and A.J. Lange, 1978, Champaign, IL: Research Press. Copyright 1978 by the authors. Adapted by permission.

We cannot let others, even unintentionally, deny the important things in our lives. If your teenager wants to use the car tonight, you may want to make time for a *shared* session of car care or suggest that the *teen* be the one to wash and vacuum it.

This may help us understand a teenager's resistance to cleaning his/her room. Parents do well to use caution in criticizing a teen's tolerance for clutter and disarray. Tolerance with respect for good health can be the goal to help a teen achieve room cleanliness.

2) You have the right to speak out and take action if you are not treated respectfully.

One father told me he met his son, Bill, talking with a group of school friends at the mall. But after Bill said, *"Hi!"* he continued his conversation with one friend instead of introducing his father. So Dad introduced himself, shaking hands with each student and talking to the nearest one.

Bill probably realized his mistake when his father took the initiative to make introductions. Later Dad can tell Bill how he felt, so next time his son will remember his responsibility. By taking action Dad showed respect for himself and set an example of how the situation could be made right.

After Bill loaned his team shirt to his sister, she left it in a heap on the floor of her room. Bill was mad. *"If you want to borrow my shirt, show some respect for it. Hang it up and return it when you're done so I'll feel like loaning you other things."* Jane knows she was wrong and is more likely to take Bill's comments seriously, because he told her what he expected instead of just demanding the shirt back.

For an exercise about respect, each person in your family could write about a situation in which he/she was not respected—not necessarily within the family. Pass the situations to the left several times. Each person can read an example and tell what action he/

Exercise 10: Values

Have each person in your family list five values they hold and two ways they carry them out every day. Pass the lists around and then each person can read the list he/she has, letting others guess who made it.

Some Suggestions for Values

achievement	good looks	marriage
recreation	animals	hobbies
mental health	religion	beauty
honesty	money	sexuality
challenge	independence	nature
social acceptance	creativity	justice
parenting	sports	ethics
learning	peace	work
friendship	loyalty	possessions
power		

The following are examples of values and ways to support them. I value...

1. My family, so I spend time doing activities with them that are fun, and I listen to them tell their experiences and explain their views.
2. Financial security, so I keep money records straight, plan purchases, and keep a budget.
3. Helping others, so I work in education and support a scholarship program.
4. My health, so I exercise regularly and eat healthy foods.
5. A clean environment, so I recycle and write letters about it.

she would do. How would other family members react? How can we call attention to the need for respect for that person?

3) You have the right to say "no" when your rights are not respected.

One mother told me about a caller who asked her to canvass the neighborhood for a charity drive. She quickly evaluated her energy limits and answered, *"No."* Time was short, and she realized she couldn't meet commitments to family and work if she took on yet another charity role. In the past, Mom had felt worn out from trying to do everything whenever anyone asked for her help. Later she focused on only the highest priorities and guarded against giving away family time. Saying *"no"* is often so difficult we have to regularly remind ourselves of priorities and rehearse our *"no"* for that next request that may come today. Family priorities are continuous and can easily slip to a lower place on the list. Parents need to guard against that temptation.

> *Saying "no" is often so difficult we have to regularly remind ourselves of priorities and rehearse our "no" for that next request that may come today.*

A teen has a right to say *"no,"* also. Laurie knew she would feel sick from the long drive to see an elderly relative; she was able to stay behind by making an alternate plan: visiting a friend's house and taking an afternoon bike ride. If the activity was *required,* Mom and Dad could still respect her feelings about the car ride by playing *her* radio station and breaking up the trip with meals. If she had been old enough, she could have driven part of the distance each way.

Priorities could be reviewed in an exercise where each family member makes a weekly time page: 7 A.M. at the top left side of a sheet of paper, and the hours down the page to 10 P.M. Across the top, list the days. Fill in daily activities and free half-hours.

Now think of one new activity you would say *"yes"* to, and one you would answer with *"no."* Share your schedules and activity choices. While some parents resent driving teens to friends' houses or tagging along on shopping trips, some do not. One father enjoyed the chance to have time alone with his teenager, confiding feelings, sharing special stories, and building a closer relationship.

4) You have the right to feel the way you do and to express your feelings.

Dad felt down when he came home from work. He'd had a run-in with an associate and other things had not gone well. Instead of trying to turn his feelings around while they ate supper, Mom and his daughters listened to his story without saying he should feel differently. They sat longer than usual around the table as each person pictured the way it was for Dad, and then told about their own day's events. Sharing the way he felt, instead of trying to cover up, helped Dad accept what had happened and look ahead.

Fourteen-year-old Chris complained, *"There's nothing to do around here!"* Mom felt he was trying to get her to play *"I-bet-you-can't-make-me-happy,"* but instead of making suggestions, she just let him know she heard him, *"You sound bored."*

"Yes, everyone's sick, and there's nothing I feel like doing."

"With everybody sick, it's hard to find something." Mom saw her teenager as growing up but still looking to her for help with the universal problem of managing time. If Chris were an adult he might have the same complaint. He had hobbies and chores that could be done, but it would take a while for him to work out an answer of his own choosing. Numerous suggestions from Mom would probably only continue an unsatisfying game of suggestions, objections, and more suggestions by Mom.

To get a better "feel for feelings," the family exercise could ask each person to share a memory, a time when he/she felt happy, angry, excited, disappointed, or some other emotion, and was accepted for having that feeling. Then they could share an incident when they were told their feelings were wrong. How did it make a difference?

5) You have the right to take time to think about choices.

If parents don't take time to consider their reactions, a teen may disrupt the family with disturbing announcements: *"I'm flunking math!" "I'm quitting band!" "I have to work in Ocean City this summer!"*

Parents need to ask themselves, *"Is the dramatic announcement a way to get into a conversation or a way to draw attention to a legitimate problem?"*

Waiting for more information may help the parent decide what is really intended. A reaction is not

> *Waiting for more information may help the parent decide what is really intended.*

necessary since these are just words, not actions.

A calm approach helps the teen think over the problem. Use listening skills to get the whole story while helping the teen examine details. When both parents are there, they should hold out for a private parent-to-parent strategy session to find a compromise, instead of allowing teens to play each parent against the other right there on the spot. If other relatives live with you, enlist their agreement too, without teens present.

Teenagers also benefit from having time to think over consequences before making choices. *"Which friend do you want to invite on the camping trip?" "What kind of birthday celebration do you want to have next month?" "What courses will you take next year?"* Given choices and time, teens can learn to take charge of their lives.

Making choices could be part of a family exercise by having each member list a decision you had to make this past week, and recall how much time you spent considering choices. Did you need more time to make a good decision? How did your choice work out?

6) You have the right to change your mind.

To coach a growing teenager requires flexibility as the teen's capabilities increase and circumstances change. One family I know didn't allow sleep-over friends for a long time because their teen, Eric, became sick and impossibly grumpy following those occasions. But as the years matured their teen, an occasional try seemed only fair.

The right to change your mind includes the right to hold to your present position, too. When teens argue for a change in rules, parents can remind them that parental limits are not the only obstacle to independence and good times. Teens are more limited by lack of education and restricted job opportunities than by parental rules. But restrictions need to be reduced as a teen demonstrates increasing responsibility and self-reliance. When Eric's sleepover problems had eased, he presented a reasonable plan to get chores and homework done so he could go on a weekend trip. He convinced his parents to change their initial negative reaction.

Teens also have a right to change their minds. Teens are learning to plan ahead and often find they make more commitments than they can keep. Danny signed up for several clubs and then had to drop out of two activities. When he didn't help with supper because of a club meeting, Dad filled in instead, and Danny made it up the next night.

A practice exercise in changing your mind could encourage

family members to share stories. When did they make an agreement and then change it? Have each person tell what happened
and how he/she felt about it.

7) You have the right to ask for what you need or want.

As all working folk know, you *won't* get what you *don't* ask
for. Some parents sacrifice for their teenagers instead of request-
ing help. Mom wanted assistance unloading and storing groceries,
but instead of asking for it, she thought, *"My teenagers are tired,
and I can do this for them."* After she finished the work she felt
worn out, and her sacrificial attitude had turned to resentment. She
might be teaching her teens to take advantage of her (by acting
tired), and she *and they* are likely to pay a price for that.

As a practice exercise here, have each person think of a time
they asked or did not ask for help to meet a need or want. How did
the experience work out, and how did the person feel about it?

8) You have the right to make mistakes.

Dad forgot to pick up Bryan after a team practice at school.
Bryan felt let down and disappointed with his father. When it
happened a second time, Dad evaluated his efforts. Lately, work
and community activities had been too demanding to allow him to
give his son the time he needed. *"Everybody makes mistakes, me
included,"* Dad said, *"but I'm going to request a replacement on
the townhouse committee and leave work at 4:30 regularly."*

Mistakes are part of living, but feeling guilty doesn't help.
When we do slip up, we can plan a change to make amends.

When her teen acted in ways Mom disliked, Mom started using
the adage, *"I like you, but not your behavior."* Then she realized
she needed to request certain actions and praise specific behaviors.
*"I made a mistake by not adding the positive expectation. Now
I'm going to try a better way."*

For an exercise about mistakes, ask each family member to share something new he/she is able to do this year that was not possible last year. Let everyone describe what made the learning possible, including mistakes.

9) You have the right to feel good about yourself.

When actions work out well, a teenager happily takes credit, like a player on a winning team, and a parent feels proud, as a winning-team coach. But when things don't work out, parents as well as teens often blame themselves for poor decisions.

Parents can set a good example for their teenager by adopting the habit of accepting credit and blame only for their own actions. A teen will learn to accept responsibility for problems as well as successes if the parent does not accept blame where there is no control. Guide the teen to connect outcomes with his/her own behaviors and not use past parent behaviors as a scapegoat.

Parents know that teens need to take the consequences for their actions themselves, but parents' feelings of embarrassment, blame, and guilt can be strong, even if others don't blame Mom or Dad. Those feelings need to be recognized, and they can be put to a useful purpose: to analyze problems and plan for changes.

For the happiness of the parent and the family, it can be a time for positive steps, to remind everyone of personal and family strengths. Put negative things in perspective by making lists of things you like about yourself and things you feel proud of. Here are a few examples.

1. I like myself because:

    I work hard, I exercise to stay healthy, I am honest, I listen to others, have activities I like to do, am faithful.

2. Things I have done that make me feel proud are:

    I helped my husband and kids, helped people at work, saved money for trips

3. Ways I have helped my family members are:
    I set an example, explored alternatives, listened,
    provided transportation, and helped plan ahead.
4. I feel proud of my family members because they are:
    caring, intelligent, honest and hard-working.

STEP 10
Seek Cooperation from
Your Spouse, Friends, and Relatives
(Single Parent, Even Double Parent, Is Often Not Enough!)

Single parents have many disadvantages in rearing children solo. Yet they do have the advantage of a more consistent set of rules and reactions. Parents with or without partners encounter new problems as child-rearing becomes *adult*-rearing. Expanding moments of separation become more apparent and the paradox of *keeping* control while also *giving it away* creates tough moments for all parents.

How Your Teens Treat You:
Family and Friends Should
Set a Good Example!

Friends should protect friends. That's obvious enough, but what happens in *your* home when your teen mistreats you? Who comes to your defense?

Let's look at this conversation with Mom, her son Kevin, and Aunt Eileen:

Kevin:	*"I'm going to watch TV now."*
Mom:	*"What about your homework?"*
Kevin:	*"Later. I've got plenty of time."*
Mom:	*"Isn't your history paper due tomorrow?"*
Kevin:	*"Mom, you don't know anything about how long that paper will take."*
Aunt Eileen:	*"Be careful how you talk to your mother. She's had many years of school. I think she knows."*
Kevin:	*"I'll do it when I'm ready."*
Aunt Eileen:	*"Well, I can't take you to soccer practice until your Mom says you are ready."*
Kevin:	*"You didn't even know about the history paper until Mom brought it up. It's none of your business."*
Mom:	*"Don't talk to your aunt that way. She's concerned about you too. Now get to that paper so you can get to your practice on time."*

This struggle may not end here, but Mom and Aunt Eileen, standing up for each other, are not going to take part in Kevin's divide-and-conquer strategy. They stay close, and they don't tolerate abuse from Kevin.

Your best protectors are your own relatives, friends, or spouse who will come to your aid when you are being mistreated—even by a child. Two adults can be stronger than one, and they can provide a model to children and teens about how members of the family should treat each other. *"Say, be careful how you speak to your mother!"* can be a source of comfort to a mom and a help to a growing teen blundering into accumulating guilt. Here's Mom with her friend Erica and her daughter Jenny:

Jenny:	*"Mom, where's my tennis racket?"*
Mom:	*"Just a minute, I'm talking."*
Jenny:	*"I need it now!"*
Erica:	*"Take it easy, Jenny, let your Mom finish."*
Mom:	*"Thanks, Erica. I can use that support now and then."*

How Does the Parent Abuse Habit Get Started?

A child's attitude comes from many sources, but relatives, friends, spouses and the extended family play a role from the beginning. They can make the effort to help, like Erica and Aunt Eileen, or, if they don't, they can be part of the problem. Here's Jane with her husband John:

John:	*"You can't find your keys? I can't believe it!"*
Jane:	*"Just a minute. Here they are."*
John:	*"I swear, you would lose your head if you didn't have…"*

An adult game of *"I-can't-believe-you're-such-a-klutz!"* can be easily absorbed by the kids, and **spouses or adult friends should avoid these "games."** No one can watch everything they say, but friends of parents, particularly friends of single parents, should keep in mind the examples they set for the children. The best help a friend of a parent can give is to show a model of respect for the one doing the parenting.

Mom and Aunt Eileen in the car with Kevin and Jenny:

> Aunt Eileen: *"If you're going to look for a new car, you better take someone with you who knows something about it."*
>
> Mom: *"I know something about it. I have three articles right here, I've read 'Buyer's Review,' and know the ratings."*
>
> Aunt Eileen: *"Oh, then you're really prepared. What do you think of these prices?"*

Aunt Eileen starts off a little negative but ends up asking Mom for information. Now, Mom needs to return the favor.

> Mom: *"How did the car you have hold up?"*

If significant others are going to help, Mom's (or Dad's) model of showing respect for the significant other needs to be part of the teen's family experience. When Mom respects the opinions of others, her example improves the value of the opinions of the others in the eyes of the kids.

Now, when friends or relatives show confidence in Mom's ability to do anything from driving to making financial decisions, their opinion bears added weight when the children hear it. *"What do you think about these prices?"* sends a message not only to Mom, as a parent, that her thoughts are of value, but also to any other ears in hearing range.

This is a good reason to sort out conflicts in private—away from the children. Children always have their "antennae out" and are more interested in what the conversations say about how *the people around them feel about each other* than the content of the argument.

> John: *"This car needs some work."*
>
> Jane: *"Why don't you take it in Monday."*
>
> John: *"Me? You're the one who drives it most!"*
>
> Jane: *"I have to get to work early. You just lounge around until 8:30 anyway."*
>
> John: *"Hey, you have a cushy job..."*
>
> Jane: *"Wait, wait, let's get the car fixed, OK?"*

Both John and Jane may think this argument is about car repairs and who should see that it gets done. But a teen listening on the side may not understand or even care about the details of dropping a car off for repairs. **The teen is listening only to the message about the opinion each person has of the other.**

So after a simple disagreement on the car, John may be surprised to hear Jenny say: *"You don't like Mom, do you?"*

> John: *"What? Of course I do. Whatever gave you that idea?"*

The misunderstanding teens get from focusing on what seems to be the feelings the adults have for each other can be corrected. But the temptation to imitate what they have heard will linger on and that can only be corrected by future examples from you— and from the Ericas, Johns, and Aunt Eileens in your family's social world.

> *Moms and Dads do not need friends or relatives around who show the children how to abuse their parents.*

All parents need the other adults around the family to show a positive model and message for the children to hear. **Moms and Dads do not need friends or relatives around who show the children how to abuse their parents.** That kind of friend or relative should be asked to begin changing their attitudes...or begin leaving.

Parental Teams

Most encounters in parenting are first-time experiences. Even parents with many children are usually surprised at what the next one does. **Parents need companion parents to create a situation that is both their sounding board and their think tank.** And we need the assurance that others have problems similar to ours.

Whether you are on your own or in partnership, a Parent Support Group can be a great help. Start a small parents group today. Even a reluctant spouse will develop some new ideas and attitudes from a discussion group. A few calls will produce other parents who are willing to be a part. Agreement on parental strategies is *not* a requirement. The opportunity to sort through common problems is the important part, and you will probably discover everyone is partly right.

For opening topics at meetings you could start with one of the steps or exercises in this book. Other topics suggested by individuals could be a part of each meeting so that each meeting covers immediate concerns. Exercise 11 at the end of this step can be a good starting point.

Waning Parental Influence

Friends in a support group see your child less often than you do. They can help you with new insights. Gradual changes taking place in a child going from 12 on up are easy to miss. We often think of our teens as being the same when changes are actually taking place every week and month!

The parent support group can help a mom or dad who, not recognizing growth, continues old limits on responsibilities and opportunities. **Timely changes would strengthen their son or daughter's always-fragile self-worth.** Parents can lose influence just by neglecting the teen's expanding areas of interest. So a teen's complaint of "nothing to do" should be taken as more than just a complaint about the lack of amusements. It could reflect a need for useful activities that are respected in his limited adult world. **One fast way to alienate a member from a group is to not allow them to contribute when they are ready to do it!**

> *One fast way to alienate a member from a group is to not allow them to contribute when they are ready to do it!*

A strange effect of sexism in our culture is that girls sometimes survive childhood better than boys because they make an earlier contribution to the family, particularly with the domestic chores. While "protecting" the male from drudgery, parents can run the risk of driving their son to find other activities that show he can "do something." **Threatened by his feeling of "worthlessness," he will cast around for a way to be proud of himself—what will he find?** Will it be a suggestion from his mom or dad? Or something not influenced by his parents and encouraged only by mischievous others?

Some competition for parental influence will come from a teen's expanding circle of friends. Parents feel obligated to hold to limits that are not always popular and so begin with a disadvantage in the competition with their son or daughter's friends. Friends are likely to reward a wide range of behavior and seldom reprimand or punish. The intolerance of peers to deviation from the accepted may seem obvious to parents, but examples of the standards are presented by every peer, making a teen's adjustment to these standards easy.

Your parental advantage is that you know how important *positive* support is, and you can plan heavy doses for good behavior for teens hungry for confirmation that they are doing right. **Positive support is the major advantage parents have in**

**the competition for influence with friends who give their
support and criticism without much thought.** But parents need
to be clear about what is worthy of support.

*"I think you're wonderful even when your friends let you
down"* is often an important role for parents, but too much of it can
be cruelly misleading preparation for the adult world. A parent
support group can be helpful here as well. How are other parents
reacting to new fads and habits? What *good* developments are they
encouraging?

Parents as Teachers, Coaches, Friends, and "Heavies"

Parental roles change with situations as well as with the ages of
the children. Parents need to be aware of these changes and avoid
feeling "inconsistent" when different roles seem to be called for.
Often a teen's confusion over Mom or Dad's changing attitudes
can be erased by a frank explanation of their mixture of
perspectives:

Jack:	*"Why can't we have the other cable channels. Everyone else has them."*
Mom:	*"They cost more money. And not everyone has them. Parents in my group also say they're too expensive."*
Jack:	*"But we're missing all the good stuff!"*
Mom:	*"You see plenty of TV with its violence and …stuff. I want you to use some of your time for useful things—where you learn something."*
Jack:	*"If you were my friend, you would get the other channels."* (Sounds like a game of *"If-you-loved-me-you-would-serve-me"*)

Mom: *"Jack, I <u>am</u> your friend, but sometimes I have to be a parent who also looks out for your future. It's not easy doing both."*

Jack: *"Well, I'd be a lot happier friend if I had the other channels."*

Mom: *"Maybe so. But I have to be the parent who watches our money and watches out for your learning, and I want to be a friend, too. It's hard."*

Does Jack understand all this about conflicting roles? I doubt it. But he does understand that Mom is trying to do the best thing even when she doesn't provide what he wants.

Jack: *"All the kids get so noisy at soccer practice. You're the coach, you should tell them to shut up!"* (Sounds like a game of *"You're-the-parent-let-me-tell-you-your-job."*)

Dad: *"Sometimes I don't want to be the heavy. If there's nothing going on at the moment, they can let go a little."*

Jack: *"I try to tell them."*

Dad: *"Hard to control the whole group. Sometimes you should try going off with a friend and just doing a little passing practice until the next drill."*

Jack: *"You're more strict with me than you are with them!"*

Dad: *"It's different. They're not my children. Sometimes I worry more over how you are doing. To them I'm only the coach. To you I'm a parent."*

A Brief Last Word

In these 10 steps, I have advocated a practical approach to adult-rearing. My philosophy is that children, teens, and adults have more similarities than we sometimes think. The most important similarities are that everyone deserves respect and room to follow their own interests.

The successful efforts of both adults and their children need recognition and support to keep the progress of learning moving forward. In the child's or teen's case the feeling of self-esteem is still developing, and positive reactions from parents are especially critical.

The justification for punishment is not strengthened by pointing out the young age or small stature of the victim. However, corrections, feedback, and a chance to make amends are in order for both adults and offspring.

Parents should gather adults around them who will help with the parenting job by respecting and confirming the parents' rights. Sometimes grandma or grandpa may need to be told,

> *"Mom (Dad), I need your respect and help with the children. It's harder for me if your remarks suggest to the children that I am not capable."*

If your spouse or a relative lives with you, it's all the more important that you show each other the respect you want from the children, and that you come to each other's defense and aid when it's needed.

Most likely your children will resemble you. **The dominating factor in how they turn out is your model for them.** This is a large responsibility to keep in mind.

But you are a natural for the job. You're the one most

interested in the welfare of your children, and you're close at hand every day. To enjoy the parenting, stick to good habits, show a good model, listen, and cultivate some close advisors to discuss problems and solutions. We humans are busy with our complex lives, but we have some extra help: we learn well from each other.

All the steps and suggestions in this book take time. Helping a child cross over the teenage years to adulthood requires time—for talking, planning, and soul-searching. Talking keeps the understanding and friendship healthy. Planning presents a clear view of the important behaviors and keeps the incentives logical and fair. And the soul-searching is for discovering the times to give over more responsibilities to a growing-up person.

Exercise 11: Team Up with Spouses, Companions, and Other Parents

Ground Rules for Discussions in Parent Support Groups

Parent Support Groups can provide a comfort and good sense of direction with the proper ground rules. They might also serve as a sort of extended family for your teen, adding a wider circle of positive adult influences and role models in his or her life.

At the first get-together, the group should take up the following ground rules and come to an understanding, if not an agreement, on how each issue will be handled.

Concerning Trust:
1. Confidentiality for companion parents.
2. Rules for telling stories about your teens and repeating stories about other parents' teens heard at group sessions.

Concerning Consideration for Others:
3. Controlling the air time.
    What is fair share?
    How will we police the air time?
    Air time on a hot topic.
4. Balancing topic time and social time.

Concerning the Topic:
5. Selecting topics
6. The group is not an individual therapy session.
7. The group is not a couples therapy session.

Concerning General Rules:

8. Degrading the kids, even your own, is not allowed.
9. Members act on their own responsibility, for example, in dealing with the schools, and do not take action in the group's name.
10. Splitting the group. Sometimes when the ground rules are ignored, radical changes are necessary for your teen's sake.

Suggestions for Discussion for a Single Parent in the Parent Support Group:

1. How do other members of the group maintain their roles as *adult* and *parent*? How do they avoid using their teen as a weapon against their former spouse or a sounding board for emotional problems. How do they remain strong, reliable, cheerful and loving for their children.

2. Is it true that no matter how conscientiously you help a teen understand the divorce or separation, at times, he/she will think it's his/her fault? How have others talked this over with their teen?

3. We want to keep our lives as stable and predictable as possible for our teens. How are other members of the group handling new adult relationships?

4. How do other members of the group avoid making an enemy of their former spouse and avoid competing with him/her. How do they work out the best interests of their teen with him/her. How can parents help their teen know that *both* his/her parents love and care about him/her.

5. How do most parents schedule meals at home for the family?

6. What other books are good on child and teen behavior? Can other parents recommend books that have effective techniques for managing key issues?

7. How have others involved themselves and their children in civic, church or community activities? Could the group also provide an extended family network for its members?

INDEX

Index

Also by the author...

Raising Good Kids in Tough Times

7 Crucial Habits for Parent Success

These 7 crucial habits help parents raise good kids, maintain a loving relationship, and counter the dangerous examples, attitudes and temptations children face in today's multimedia world. Practical guidelines are illustrated with over 200 examples and more than 60 parent-child dialogues. This book covers the basics from toilet training, sleeping habits, and listening skills to sibling rivalry, sex, drugs, and social skills. It also addresses single-parent problems and strategies and parent activism in the school and community.

What reviewers say...

> *"...readable, well-organized and full of sensible advice for parents...fresh help to parents... timing could not be better."*
> —Foreword Magazine

> *"These are the habits parents need for confidence and the ones that can help in times of trouble."*
> —Dr. Donald Pumroy, Founder of Assn. for Behavior Change, Prof. Emeritus, Univ. of MD.

ISBN 0-9640558-9-9 • $14.95